All Hail the Power of Jesus' Name

The History of Christ Cathedral

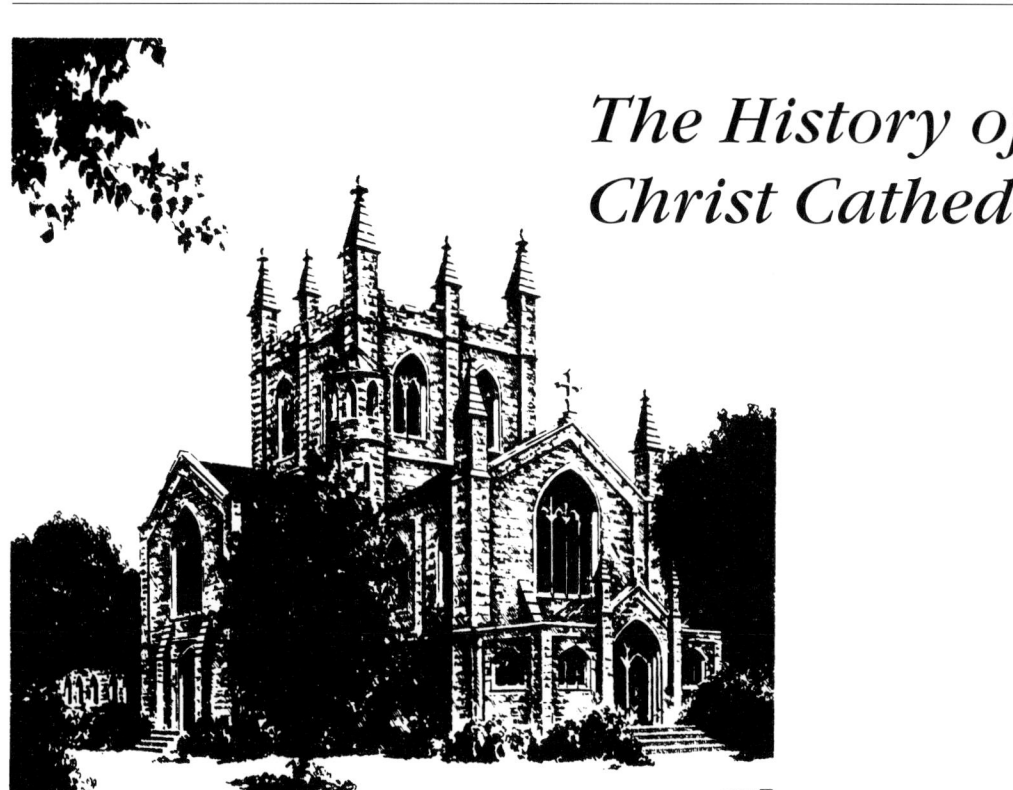

Copyright © 1992 by Christ Cathedral. 138 South Eighth Street, Salina, Kansas 67401

All Rights reserved. No part of this book may be reproduced, stored in a retrieval system, or transmitted in any form or by any means, electronic, mechanical, photocopying, recording, or otherwise, without the prior permission of Christ Cathedral.

Library of Congress Catalog No. 92-74822

ISBN No. 0-9635141-0-5

Printed in U.S.A. by Mennonite Press, Inc., Newton, Kansas 67114

To the glory of God

FOREWORD

What is a cathedral? The word "cathedral" conjures up for many people a picture of huge gothic churches, with heavy stone vaults hanging high above, supported by soaring arches, and adorned with flying buttresses, gargoyles, and massive brilliantly colored windows. Grand ceremonies come to mind, with colorful processions winding down a long nave to the rumble of a majestic organ and the ethereal sounds of a boy choir.

But this is a romantic, and not altogether accurate, picture. Some cathedrals are gothic, but not all — Sir Basil Spence's marvelous modern Cathedral Church of Saint Michael in Coventry, England, comes immediately to mind. Some cathedrals are huge, but not all — the first cathedral in the Episcopal Church, the Cathedral of Our Merciful Saviour in Faribault, Minnesota, is no larger than an ordinary parish church, but is no less a cathedral. These are not the things that make a church a cathedral.

What, then, is a cathedral? It is the word itself which tells us the main thing we need to know. The distinguishing mark of a cathedral is a piece of furniture, the *cathedra,* the chair of the bishop. A cathedral is that church which houses the chair of the bishop of a diocese. Thus, a cathedral is the bishop's church and a symbol of his ministry. The first Bishop of Albany, one of the pioneers in the cathedral movement in this country, once said, "I consider no episcopate complete that has not a center, the cathedral, as well as a circumference, the Diocese." Curiously enough, when William Croswell Doane spoke those words in 1868 there were only four or five cathedrals in the whole Episcopal Church, but something new was happening, and in time Salina would be part of the story.

When the first Anglicans came to these shores nearly four hundred years ago, they lacked something essential — essential, at least, if catholic faith and order are taken seriously. They had laypeople. They had priests. They had the Book of Common Prayer and, of course, the English Bible. But they had no bishops. For more than one hundred seventy-five years, Anglicans in America were presided over by absentee bishops, the successive Bishops of London, not one of whom ever set foot in the colonies. To be confirmed, one had to go to England. To be ordained, one had to go to England. Few colonists ever even saw a bishop; fewer still ever received any sacrament from the hands of a bishop. As for the ministry of the bishop as guardian and teacher of the faith, pastor of his people, sign of unity — these things were completely unknown on this side of the Atlantic.

This long famine of episcopal presence certainly had an impact. It has been suggested that the Church in the colonies had managed so long without bishops that when some finally turned up no one knew what to do with them — or cared. There had certainly been no hurry to obtain bishops: the first was elected in 1783 and consecrated the following year; the next two were not consecrated until 1787. The early bishops remained rectors of parish churches, having a limited episcopal ministry. And none thought of having a cathedral (or even of calling his parish church by that title).

It was the catholic revival which brought the cathedral idea to the fore. And that is hardly surprising. It is the catholic vision of the Church which holds before us its unity in mission and ministry. It is the catholic vision of the Church which sees the order of the Church as something essential to its life and not just a convenient or efficient form of organization. Thus, it is the catholic vision of the Church which understands that the bishop really must be at the center of the life of the Church. St. Ignatius of Antioch wrote at the beginning of the second century, "Wherever the bishop appears, there is the whole community (i.e., the Church); just as wherever Jesus Christ is, there is the catholic Church."

The catholic understanding of the Church as a mystical body, a divinely constituted fellowship, rather than human institution, nevertheless sees a man at the center, a sacramental person whose identity transcends his individuality. It is Ignatius, again, who says that the bishop is "a type of the Father."

As the Church grew, and particularly as it was no longer possible for the whole Church in one city to gather in one church building, bishops were obliged to move around to minister to their people. But the bishop's central position in the Church came to be represented by a particular church, the church in which his chair (the chair of the apostolic teacher) was set. And it was not just an empty building when the bishop was absent. Within it prayer for and with the bishop carried on daily, whether or not he was present. Cathedrals became great centers of education, representing the teaching ministry which is central to the apostolic office. They became centers of mission, again extending the apostolic work of the bishop.

The genius of the cathedral idea in America recognized the unique role of the cathedral in a new way, pioneered in Albany and reflected in Salina. In these and in other cathedrals, even the institutional structure of the cathedral held up the central role of the bishop in relationship to the whole Church. The bishop himself, not a rector, presides over the Chapter which governs the Cathedral,. The other members of the Chapter are drawn not only from the clergy and laity of the cathedral parish, but from the clergy and laity of the bishop's whole diocese. As the cathedral idea came out of the catholic revival, it should not be surprising that it holds up in an intentional way the catholic vision of the Church as one body centered in one person, as the catholic Church is one Body in Christ.

It would seem to be more than mere coincidence that this history of Christ Cathedral in Salina is being published in the year in which another catholic institution celebrates the one hundred fiftieth anniversary of her founding. Nashotah House, the catholic seminary of the Episcopal Church, was founded by men of a catholic and missionary mind in that moment of history when the catholic revival was just beginning to spread in the Episcopal Church. There has been a wonderful fellowship between these two centers of faith and mission since the founding of the Cathedral. No less than three of her deans, including the present one, have been "sons of the House;" and their lives have touched and been mutually supportive in a variety of other ways.

Some see the Church, and more particularly the catholic faith, in great danger as this century ends—and they are in some degree correct. Nevertheless, the year 1992 is a moment of promise as great catholic institutions like Christ Cathedral and Nashotah House are renewed and carry on their witness. This history is a most welcome testimony to the roots of that renewal in Salina.

Gary W. Kriss
Dean of Nashotah House and
sometime Dean of Albany
September 1992

Table of Contents

I.	The Church Comes to Salina	2
II.	The Battersons	8
III.	Laying of the Cornerstone	14
IV.	Behind the Red Doors	20
	Color Photographs	35
V.	Deans	43
VI.	Bishops	66
	Color Photographs	79
VII.	Friends Around Town	87
VIII.	Inside the Walls	99
IX.	The Later Days	109
Appendix A.	Memorials	117
Appendix B.	Ordinations	124
Appendix C.	Wardens	126
	Resources	128
	Contributors	130

INTRODUCTION

On 29 May 1906 a procession was formed at Christ Church and moved across the street to the new Cathedral site for the laying of the cornerstone. The first hymn sung on this site was "All Hail the Power of Jesus' Name". This new Cathedral was the dream of The Right Reverend Sheldon Munson Griswold and it was made possible by the generosity of Mrs. Sarah Elizabeth Batterson of Philadelphia. The Cathedral was a memorial to her late husband, The Reverend Hermon Griswold Batterson, who as rector of St. Clement's Church, Philadelphia, made a strong Anglo-Catholic witness suffering unjust attacks by low churchmen and bishops in his day.

The Battersons were deeply committed to the Catholic revival within Anglicanism. It is this movement which restored to Anglicans many of the outward signs which we enjoy and often take for granted at Christ Cathedral. The Anglo-Catholic wing of the Episcopal Church was in a confident mood when the cornerstone was being laid in 1906 and this new Cathedral was a symbol of their confidence.

Christ Cathedral became an expression — in stone, wood and glass — of the glory of God and the dignity and creativity of man. The building of the Cathedral is a marvelous testimony to the faith and determination of the early Episcopalians in Salina and our Diocese. In this book, we will attempt to tell their story.

Many attempts have been made in the past to make this cathedral history a reality. Joyce White, during her time as Cathedral Archivist gathered together a wealth of information. John Q. Royce continued her work after she left Salina. After John's death in late 1991, Jo Reed and Canon Joseph Kimmett took up the challenge and have labored mightily to see this effort through to publication. We thank them and the many hands and minds which have made contributions to this Cathedral history.

This book stands as a record of our past. As we read it and re-discover our rich heritage, pray that we might also find encouragement to faith and the confidence of our Anglo-Catholic forebearers and benefactors that we in our day will continue to sing "All Hail the Power of Jesus' Name."

The Very Reverend
M. Richard Hatfield, S.T.M.

I. THE CHURCH COMES TO SALINA

Now the eleven disciples went to Galilee, to the mountain to which Jesus had directed them. And when they saw him they worshiped him; but some doubted. And Jesus came and said to them, "All authority in heaven and on earth has been given to me. Go therefore and make disciples of all nations, baptizing them in the name of the Father and of the Son and of the Holy Spirit, teaching them to observe all that I have commanded you; and lo, I am with you always, to the close of the age." — Matthew 28:16-20

A few short years after the War of the American Revolution ended, many of the same men who framed the Constitution of the United States came together again in Philadelphia where they put their signatures to the papers which formally organized the Episcopal Church. Fifty years down the road, The Right Reverend Jackson Kemper became the first bishop of the Church to visit the Kansas territory. Sent out from New York, his hardy band of missionaries stopped in Fort Leavenworth in 1837. Twenty-seven years later, in 1864, the Diocese of Kansas was formed and the Right Reverend Thomas Vail was elected its first bishop. It was four short years later the first missionary was sent to Salina.

The Right Reverend Thomas H. Vail, First Bishop of Kansas

The town of Salina was established in 1858 by Colonel W.A. Phillips and his party from Lawrence, Kansas. The Civil War deterred much growth until the Union Pacific Railway entered the scene in 1867. Pioneers came to settle the prairie lands from all parts of the country. Those from the eastern and southern states brought with them a tradition of worship known as that of the Episcopal Church. In 1868, ten years after its birth as a community, the first Episcopal services were held in Salina.

Among the first clergymen to visit Salina was The Reverend C.E. Griffith who came from Topeka, Kansas to investigate the possibility of introducing the Church. During his visit in 1868 he found so few people interested in the Church, that he deemed it unwise to attempt any sort of formal organization. It was Father Griffith though, in that same year who officiated at the first baptism in Salina. The story is told of a Mrs. James Sharpe, who upon hearing that an Episcopal priest was to be in the district, brought her children from their home, "a distance in the country", to be baptized by Griffith. Her daughter, Anne Griffith Sharpe, born in September 1866, was the first known person to receive the sacrament, taking her middle name from the man who christened her.

Griffith held services in a cabin for about six weeks, before leaving Salina. During the next year, services were held on occasions when a priest was available. The man who would cover Salina on and off for may years was The Reverend J.H. Lee, rector of St. Paul's Church in Manhattan, Kansas. Lee was also the Professor of Languages at the State Agricultural College in Manhattan. In the Spring of 1870, The Reverend Dr.

Reynolds, chaplain at Fort Riley, an army post about fifty miles east of Salina, also visited Salina and held Sunday services which were well attended.

While it would still be some time before Salina would have its own priest, the laity gathered to begin organizing a congregation. Nineteen families committed themselves to the effort, among them eleven confirmed communicants, including Mrs. J.H. Prescott, sister of Father Lee and Mr. Richard J. Watson in whose general merchandise store the group met. Mr. Watson's store was located on lot #98 on North Santa Fe, where Vernon Jewelers is now located. An old history describes meetings of the congregations in a vivid way — some were seated on kegs, one or two on chairs, others on coils of rope, counters and whatever else could be converted into a seat.

The group moved quickly and on April 12, 1870, they completed their organizational work and elected a vestry. Mr. James Chase and Mr. J.H. Prescott were chosen wardens, and Messrs. H.M. Clarkson, H.B. Merrell, C.S. Loverin, C.A. Hiller, and R.J. Watson were elected to serve as vestrymen. Arrangements were made to hold services every two weeks at the newly-completed Baptist church at Eighth and Ash Streets.

In May 1870, Diocesan Convention was held in Junction City and the congregation from Salina was admitted to the Diocese of Kansas and given the title Christ Church. From the very beginning, the congregation was self-supporting. Among those who made up the core of the congregation were E.E. Bowen, Mr. and Mrs. James Chase, Mr. and Mrs. W.M. Clarkson, Mrs. Marcena Coburn, M.A. Fassett, Mr. Frank Goodnow, C.A. Hiller, Miss Mary Keith, Miss Nellie Keith, Dr. and Mrs. J.K. Lull, Mr. and Mrs. C.L. Loverin, Mr. and Mrs. H.B. Merrill, Mr. and Mrs. J.H. Prescott, Mr. and Mrs. G.C. Robert, and Mr. and Mrs. R.J. Watson. On July 3, 1870, the first full time priest was sent to Christ Church, The Reverend C. Kinney Hull.

The congregation was now meeting at the recently finished Presbyterian church on South Eighth Street. In 1871, the parishioners of Christ Church purchased lot #127 which sat on the east side of Eighth Street between Iron and Walnut. There they erected the first Episcopal church in the city, completed in 1872. It was small frame church built primarily through the generosity of Mr. Frank Goodnow, a vestryman and lumber dealer. The structure was dedicated by Father Hull.

Hull left Salina in 1873 and the vestry called The Reverend Thomas B. Dooley to succeed him. The story is told that Father Dooley came to Salina, along with Bishop Vail to confer with the vestry. After considerable conversation, Father Dooley remarked, "Lift your mortgage so the church can be consecrated, and I will come." At that, Mr. Goodnow jumped to his feet and in an excited voice exclaimed, "It is lifted now." and pulling from his pocket a note for $300.00 due to himself, he tore it in two and a touched a match to the pieces. True to his word, Dooley came to Salina, moving his family from Pontiac, Michigan, where he had been rector for twenty-one years. They arrived in Salina in October 1874. The church was consecrated the following summer, a week after Trinity Sunday.

At the Diocesan Convention in 1875, Dooley reported the following information about the Episcopal Church in Salina:

The first Episcopal Church in Salina, Christ Church, 127 South Eighth Street, could boast a bell tower.

Easter Sunday at Christ Church, 127 South Eighth Street, Salina.

Families — 35
Individuals — 49
Communicants — 25
Baptisms — 48
Confirmations — 4
Marriages — 1
Burials — 16
Sunday School — 2 teachers and 14 scholars
Contributions — $521.45
Outside contributions — $543.85

In the course of giving the report, Dooley said, "Out of debt, our church painted and carpeted, and above all, consecrated to the holy worship of the Triune God. Our hearts are made to rejoice in the hope of a sustaining and merciful Christ, the giver of all blessings." Father Dooley faithfully served the parish until his death in August 1881.

There was an interim of several months during which The Reverend J.H. Young, a priest of the Diocese of New York, served Christ Church. The vestry then elected the Reverend Peter Wager as rector. He arrived in Salina in 1883 from Ellsworth, Kansas, a town some thirty miles to the west of Salina where he had been vicar. He had also been covering St. George's Church in Victoria, Kansas, about ninety miles to the west. Some of the first Anglican liturgies in Kansas were held in Victoria, a town originally settled by English immigrants, but which was later occupied by German Roman Catholics. In addition to his charge in Salina, Wager was also assigned to cover McPherson to the south and Minneapolis to the north and so Christ Church was again without regular Sunday services. Wager and his family were plagued with illness and tragedy, losing a son who drowned in a nearby river. These and other circumstances contributed to a decline in attendance and enthusiasm during Wager's years in Salina.

In October 1886, the vestry, consisting of Messrs. Culp, Watson, Prescott, Simcock and Hogben made a call to The Reverend Joseph A. Antrim of Beloit, a town to the north of Salina, to come as rector of Christ Church. Father Antrim was offered a salary of $1200.00 per year along with the assurance that a rectory would be built. Antrim was a man of high energy and solid leadership; under his guidance the church was repaired and enlarged – the transepts, a chancel, vestry room, vestibule and a tower were all added. The Knights Templar of Salina donated an oak altar in memory of Father and Mrs. Dooley. The rectory was built at 141 South Eighth under the direction of Mr. Hugh King, an architect and builder. According to the 1887 parochial report, Antrim had the parish purchase 40 acres of land, (valued at $800.00 per acre,) plus they acquired $3200.00 for the building of a church school. Antrim, however, resigned in October 1887 to accept a call to St. George's, Leadville, Colorado.

During the interim, the parish was led by the church wardens, Mr. R.J. Watson and Mr. Hugh King, as well as the missionary, Father J.H. Lee. The next year, The Reverend E.P. Chittenden, a member of the Seabury Divinity School faculty accepted a call as Rector of both Christ Church and the newly-founded St. John's School. He arranged his first visit to Salina in March of 1888 in order to conduct the Holy Week and Easter liturgies, even though he wouldn't receive a salary until April. While in Salina, Chittenden taught at St. John's and edited *The Sentinel*, the only Episcopal Church paper published in the Diocese at the time. He resigned in the Fall of 1891.

After several months without a priest, the parish called The Reverend E. DeLongy as rector. He served Christ Church for six years. In 1892 he presented a confirmation class of eleven which included his son, Fred Maurice. His daughter, Eshet Lilian was one of four in the confirmation class of 1894. Following DeLongy, the vestry called The Reverend Irving Baxter as rector. Father Baxter came to Salina from the Diocese of Nebraska and began his work on All Saints Day 1897. He resigned early in 1901 to take a position at the University of Kansas in Lawrence.

The eighth priest to serve Christ Church would also become the first dean of Christ Cathedral, though it would be some years before there was a cathedral building or dean's stall. That priest was The Reverend William R. McKim.

As the state's population enlarged, a decision was made at the Diocesan Convention of 1901 to divide the dio-

The Right Reverend Frank R. Millspaugh, Third Bishop of Kansas.

cese. The Bishop of Kansas, The Right Reverend Frank R. Millspaugh took the idea to the General Convention of the Episcopal Church, meeting in San Francisco that year, and the Missionary District of Salina was born. The new missionary district, covering the western two thirds of the state was to be under control of General Convention.

On January 8, 1903, The Reverend Sheldon M. Griswold, Rector of Christ Church, Hudson, New York, was consecrated as the first bishop for the Missionary District. A month later, Griswold made his first trip west. As he alighted from the train in Salina, he made the decision that this town would be his See City. The bishop was well received by the priest and people of Christ Church. The facilities on Eighth Street were offered to Griswold as a pro-cathedral, but the bishop had other ideas. Griswold shared his dream of a cathedral, built on the English pattern, including the organization of a cathedral chapter.

On April 13, at the Annual Parish Meeting, the people of Christ Church unanimously asked the bishop to proceed. By reorganizing the vestry into a chapter, not only would members of the local parish have input, but representatives of the missionary district as well. The Chapter was incorporated on 30 June 1903; members included the Bishop, Messrs. E.W. Staples, J. Dedman, T.B. Seitz, A.L. Keith, C.A. Lee and Dr. J.H. Winterbotham, all of Salina, and the Honorable Houston Whiteside of Hutchinson.

In July of 1903, the Chapter met at the home of Bishop Griswold and adopted a constitution and bylaws. Father McKim, the incumbent rector was elected Dean. The Reverend R.H. Mize, Rector of St. John's School was elected Canon and The Reverend J.H. Lee, the pioneer missionary was elected Honorary Canon. Mr. Simcock was elected registrar and Mr. Seitz as treasurer. The former vestry deeded their property to the newly formed Chapter, including all debts and liabilities.

Two interesting notes from 1905 shed light on the progress of the the young Cathedral and Missionary District. A report from Easter day shows splendid attendance at the services; a remark in the service register states that chairs had to be placed in the aisle and only three seats went unused. However, evidence in the annual report of the Missionary District, printed in the National Church's *Domestic Report*, would leave a modern Christian questioning the goals of growth: Of $6000 allocated to the District for Mission work, $3300 went to the bishop for support and traveling expense and $2700 went for "mission work among white people."

In under forty years, Episcopalians in Salina had moved from sitting on coils of rope in the general store to making preparations for the building of a cathedral. They had gone from the days when priestly service was sporadic at best, to a time when both a bishop and dean would reside within the city limits. On the frontier of America, the transformation from trading post and buffalo land was made, and the faithful were determined to carry out the work of God.

II. The Battersons

Of this gospel I was made a minister according to the gift of God's grace which was given me by the working of his power. To me, though I am the very least of all the saints, this grace was given, to preach to the Gentiles the unsearchable riches of Christ, and to make all men see what is the plan of the mystery hidden for ages in God who created all things; that through the church the manifold wisdom of God might now be made known to the principalities and powers in the heavenly places. This was according to the eternal purpose which he has realized in Christ Jesus our Lord, in whom we have boldness and confidence of access through our faith in him.
— Ephesians 3:7-12

No history of Christ Cathedral would be complete, indeed no history could even begin without the Battersons. The stately English gothic structure on South Eighth Street is a gift in memory of The Reverend Hermon Griswold Batterson, by his wife, Sarah Elizabeth Batterson. When Mrs. Batterson gave the money to build the cathedral, her ideals were simple; she wanted to build a House of God where all people would be welcome and where prayers would rise daily to Almighty God. The inscription on the plaque in the rear of the nave, dedicating the cathedral reads:

*With the condition that the seats shall be forever free and unassigned, this cathedral church is built to the glory of God for the use of his people.
In loving memory of
Hermon Griswold Batterson,
priest, May 9 A.D. 1903.
Of your charity pray for his soul,
God grant him the light
of his presence with the everlasting peace of his heavenly kingdom.*

Father Batterson was born February 6, 1827, in Bloomfield, Connecticut. He was the fourth of thirteen children born to Simeon and Milissa (Roberts) Batterson. Simeon's sister Laura married a man named Harvey Griswold in 1822, and though it cannot be stated with any certainty, it is likely the young Batterson took his middle name from his aunt and uncle who served as godparents at his baptism. Little is known about his early life or his education. He most likely studied privately for the priesthood.

At the age of 34 he was ordained deacon by The Right Reverend Alexander Gregg of Texas. He served as a missionary for eighteen months, first in Sequin,

The Reverend Hermon Griswold Batterson, in whose memory Christ Cathedral was built.

Texas, then at St. Mark's in San Antonio. In the Fall of 1862, Batterson moved to Minnesota where he was given charge of Grace Church, Wabashaw and where he was ordained to the sacred priesthood by The Right Reverend Henry B. Whipple in 1866. In May of that year he resigned from Grace Church and moved to Philadelphia, though he maintained his canonical residence in Minnesota.

In October of 1866, Batterson married Sarah Elizabeth Farnum in her home parish of St. James the Less, Philadelphia. The officiant was The Right Reverend Robert Clarkson, first bishop of Nebraska. For the next two years Father Batterson worked for the Society for the Increase of Ministry, an organization which helped and supported young men in seminary training.

Batterson accepted a call to St. Clement's, Philadelphia, in 1869 and at that time transferred his canonical residence to the Diocese of Pennsylvania. St. Clement's had a grand reputation as a high church, Anglo-Catholic parish. The Episcopal Church at that time was embroiled in a battle over ritual: the use of candles, vestments, incense. Father Batterson himself became involved in the controversy, but, in the end, left the parish quite strong. In recognition of his determination and zeal, the Nebraska Divinity School of Nebraska City awarded him the degree, Doctor of Divinity. Batterson's churchmanship was also evident in that he once served as Superior of the American Branch of the Confraternity of the Blessed Sacrament.

Several serious health problems forced Batterson to resign from St. Clement's in 1872. He moved from Philadelphia and spent the next eight years away from parish work. In 1880 he returned to Philadelphia, accepting a call as Rector of the Church of the Annunciation. He remained there until 1888. Again, he left parochial work, but in 1891 accepted a call to the Church of the Redeemer in New York City. He retired from that parish and spent several years traveling abroad.

Father Batterson died in New York on March 9, 1903, at the age of 76. The burial office and Requiem Mass were celebrated in St. John's Chapel of Trinity Church, New York. Two of the officiating priests accompanied his remains to Philadelphia where committal took place in the church yard of St. James the Less. He was described by a long time friend and priest as "a thorough and consistent Anglo-Catholic, unfeignedly loyal to the standards of our Communion, true to its ideals, unaffected by Roman longings, convinced of and content with our position. His Churchmanship was plainly illustrated by the sound sensible Catholic minds which he shaped and trained."

Batterson was well known for his literary achievements, including *A Sketchbook of the American Episcopate*, a devotional manual titled *Pathway of Faith* and two books of poetry, *Christmas Carols* and *Vesper Bells*. He edited *A Manual of Plainsong* which facilitated the use of Gregorian chant for the Psalter. He also put together the *Churchman's Hymn Book*, one of the first hymnals for the Church, published in 1869.

When Christ Cathedral was consecrated in May, 1908, The Reverend George McClellan Fiske, D.D., rector of St. Stephen's, Providence, Rhode Island, preached a sermon in memory of Batterson. He said at one point,

Christian people of the Missionary District of Salina, it is no blind chance which writes among you so imperishably the hallowed name of this Worker together with God. Little did he suspect, as, worn-out with years and infirmities and with long service in the Sacred Ministry of the Church Militant, he resigned his soul into the hands of God, the work which the spell of his name and spirit was to do here in this midland field of the great American Church. The Prince of the Catholic Church, Jesus Christ our Lord, has committed to your loving guardianship the example and the memory of this His own faithful martyr. Would that I might so speak of him who has so become the instrument of God's glory, that you might cherish him thus portrayed as one known and alive to you.

ALL HAIL THE POWER OF JESUS' NAME 11

The Right Reverend Sheldon Griswold, first bishop of the Missionary District of Salina.

One might say that it was divine providence that brought The Right Reverend Sheldon Griswold and Mrs. Sarah Elizabeth Batterson together. At the very least it was good fortune. At the suggestion of Fr. Fiske, they met in Philadelphia shortly after Fr. Batterson's death. The bishop was looking for benefactors for a cathedral on the plains of Kansas and a rather wealthy Mrs. Batterson was searching for a suitable memorial for her husband. Little is known of Mrs. Batterson's life; she was though, a most loving and supportive wife, sharing the same Anglo-Catholic tendencies as her husband. In addition to her enormous generosity to the faithful of Salina, she was also a regular contributor and benefactress to Nashotah House, the Anglo-Catholic seminary west of Milwaukee, Wisconsin, and a hospital named in honor of Bishop Clarkson. A laudable account of her is found in the transcript of the address given by Bishop Griswold to the Annual Convocation of the Missionary Diocese of Salina in May, 1916, a year after her death.

It has not been our custom to make any special comment upon the life and work of any of our people who have been called to their rest. This morning, I am constrained to depart from this custom because it is my duty to make a public record of the loss which we have sustained in the death of our chief benefactor, Sarah Elizabeth Batterson. To no one person under God do we owe more than to this good friend who was called to her rest on June 27, 1915. For twelve years, Mrs. Batterson not only contributed largely of her means, but had given intelligent interest to all of our work and constant prayer for God's blessing upon it.

During her long life, Mrs. Batterson was interested in all the good works of the Church, and more especially in the domestic missionary field. At an early date she was a supporter of The Reverend James Lloyd Breck in his pioneer work in Minnesota, in Wisconsin [where he was a founder of Nashotah House], and his work among the Indians; and also of Bishop Clarkson who first had charge of Nebraska and Dakota.

The story of the building of this cathedral where we are meeting today has never been told publicly, and there-

fore I here put upon record the following facts: Mrs. Batterson was first interested in our field through the suggestion of The Reverend Fr. and Mrs. George McClellan Fiske of Rhode Island. Just before I was returning home in the autumn of 1903, Dr. Fiske telegraphed that Mrs. Batterson would be glad to see me to learn more of our special need. It seemed to me that the one thing in a material way which was most desirable was a good church building in our See City, and I therefore asked Mrs. Batterson to give us ten or fifteen thousand dollars for the purpose.

After talking of the matter for about an hour she said, 'I will give you twenty-five thousand dollars to build it in memory of Dr. Batterson with the condition that the seats should always be free and that the Holy Eucharist should be celebrated upon all Sundays and Holy Days.' As both conditions were merely part of our plan and purpose, I had no hesitation in accepting them...

Shortly afterwards, Mrs. Batterson wrote me that she thought twenty-five thousand would be insufficient, and she would make it thirty-five thousand; and as a matter of fact eventually she sent something more than fifty thousand for the purpose. From that time forward her gifts to our work have been continuous.

It was to our great joy that Mrs. Batterson was present at the time of the consecration of this cathedral building, and she then said 'Let nothing be said about me, for I want this to be entirely a gift to God.' But now I deem it entirely proper that I should say a few words connecting this very remarkable woman whom it has been my privilege to know so well.

Mrs. Batterson had a keen mind, which she kept until the last moment of her long life, and she had an intelligent interest, not merely in the affairs of the past as often happens with old people, but in the current interest both of Church and State, and was well informed by constant reading and study, as well as by extensive travel. She was a lady of great culture and refinement, belonging to a well-known Philadelphia family, where not only ample means, but leisure for the courtesies of life created an atmosphere in which all the finer relationships of human intercourse were best developed.

It is, however, as a Christian churchwoman that I like to think of our friend, and as I most want, that you should know of her. Even at this time I would not draw aside the veil of her interior devotion were I able to do so, and it is enough to say that her life was held with Christ in God. Straight and severe in dealing with herself, she was most generous toward the faults of others. Intensely loyal to the Faith, and accepting and practicing the whole of the Catholic religion, she was most charitable in word and even in thought toward those of other faiths, and of less clear vision, and of less firm grasp upon the fundamentals of the Christian religion. The end of her mortal life came as she would have wished it, among friends, and speedily though not suddenly, for she was fortified on her last journey by the Blessed Sacrament, and she breathed her last as a priest of God uttered the blessing of God upon her.

In Mrs. Batterson's original will over sixty beneficiaries were listed, half of which were directly related to the Church. The Confraternity of the Blessed Sacrament, The Guild of All Souls, Nashotah House and Bishop Griswold were among those receiving substantial gifts. Mrs. Batterson's generosity to the work of the Cathedral also extended beyond her death. In her will she left her jewelry to Christ Cathedral. Under the direction of Bishop Griswold a communion service was commissioned using diamonds, rubies and sapphires, The set includes a chalice, paten, ciborium, lavabo bowl and two cruets. The various pieces are used to this day on Christmas, Easter, major holy days and on Sundays outside of Lent. In her will she also wrote the following concerning the Cathedral: "The Holy Communion shall always be celebrated on every Sunday, Holyday, and Saint's day; and, so soon as said Bishop [Griswold] or his successor in said office shall deem it possible, to do so on every day throughout the year, excepting, however, Good Friday."

While Father Batterson may have traveled through the Kansas territory on his journeys from Nebraska, to Texas and then to Minnesota, it is known that Mrs. Batterson was in Salina only once, and that was for the consecration of the Cathedral on Ascension Day, 1908 (May 28). Their examples of devotion to our Lord and commitment to the Faith are quite enviable and every person who walks into Christ Cathedral should be made aware of the wonderful love they have for God. Whether one stops and reads the Batterson plaque in the nave or walks behind the high altar, there will be found a humble inscription asking prayers for the faithful departed. Visitors to Salina express in remarkably similar words, their joy at discovering such a gem in the middle of Kansas. The Cathedral is indeed one of Salina's most remarkable treasures.

III. Laying of the Cornerstone

I was glad when they said to me, "Let us go to the house of the Lord." Now our feet are standing within your gates, O Jerusalem.
— Psalm 122:1-2

ALL HAIL THE POWER OF JESUS' NAME

"*Christ Cathedral in Salina, Kansas is undoubtedly one of the loveliest examples of ecclesiastical architecture in the West. It is a source of genuine satisfaction and inspiration to behold such a dignified and memorable house of God in a small city of the Great Plains country. Both in its organization and building, the Cathedral has had an interesting history"*
— The Very Reverend
Hewitt. B. Vinnedge, Ph.D., Dean
The Cathedral Age,
Winter, 1936-1937

The late nineteenth and early twentieth century provided Salina with some proud moments for all the residents and particularly the Episcopalians. The young town, still establishing itself as a place to be reckoned with, officially became a city in 1870 by action of the Kansas Legislature and the town's Board of Trustees. But according to the rules of England, it would be over three decades before Salina could distinguish itself as a city. For in Great Britain, only locations with a Church of England (Anglican / Episcopal) cathedral, can be called cities. Using those guidelines on the plains of Kansas, Salina met the standards on Tuesday, May 29, 1906 when the cornerstone of Christ Cathedral was laid. The Salina Evening Journal gave this account on the following day:

The impressive service of laying the corner stone of Christ Cathedral was held yesterday afternoon. The corner stone was covered last evening with several other stones and the building will be pushed to completion as rapidly as possible. A large force of men are doing the stone work of the building and the frames of several of the windows have already been raised. It is hoped that the building may be completed early next year.

The hope of an early completion was not realized, but the stories of the dedication ceremony and work itself are impressive. From the newspaper account come many details of that corner stone ceremony. The stone was laid in place by Bishop Sheldon Griswold of the Missionary Diocese. Assisting him were two other bishops: The Right Reverend A.L. Williams, Bishop Coadjutor of Nebraska, who was also the preacher, and Bishop Frank Millspaugh, Bishop of Kansas. Clergy of the District, along with members of the Chapter, were seated on a platform within the walls; parishioners and friends filled the yard. Musicians were seated on the porch of the Guild House at 128 South Eighth, singing and playing piano, violin, coronet, piccolo and clarinet.

The procession from the old building to the new site was led by a crucifer, a cadet of St. John's Military School and included the contractors, the architect and others. Clergy in the procession carried the level, a square, the mallet and plumb line. The hymn "All Hail the Power of Jesus' Name" was joyfully sung as the procession crossed the street. The service itself consisted mostly of hymns,

Cornerstone

Scripture readings and dedicatory prayers.

In his address, Bishop Williams summarized the growth of Salina since 1875 and remarked on the work of the Church which lay ahead. He also spoke of his early years working on the railroad in Colorado, a time when the Faith wasn't important to him. When his health failed he was sent to Philadelphia and by chance entered the doors of a church. It was there he heard a sermon which profoundly stirred him — a sermon preached by Father H.G. Batterson. At that point he dedicated his life to God and now had come to Salina to pay tribute to the priest in whose honor the cathedral was to be built. He concluded his sermon with these words:

This is to be not only a parish church, but the mother church of all this district. It is to be the center of missionary enterprise in the district. Here shall the bishop gather the clergy together, and from here shall go words of counsel; here the doors will always be open and from here will go offers of a better life. Here the truths of our holy religion shall be symbolized in song and prayer, and here man shall be taught that life consisteth not in the abundance of things which he possesseth. May this holy influence radiate from this church, and may God be with you.

Part of the liturgy included placing special items within the foundation stone. Articles included a Bible; the Book of Common Prayer; a hymnal; the private communion set used by Father Thomas Dooley, the first rector of Christ Church; three books written by Father Batterson; photographs of Batterson and Bishop Griswold; current issues of various church publications and the Salina newspapers; the sermon preached by the Bishop of Albany at Bishop Griswold's consecration (and whose diocese also served as mother diocese to Salina); various historical notes; a list of parish communicants; the American flag and a cross. At the conclusion, Bishop Griswold, with help from the builder, capped the stone and prayed:

In the name of the Father, and of the Son, and of the Holy Ghost. Amen. We lay this corner stone of the cathedral church of the Missionary District of Salina, in pious memory of The Reverend Hermon Griswold Batterson, priest and doctor; to be known as Christ Cathedral, to the honor of our Lord and Savior; that here true faith, with the fear of God and brotherly love may forever flourish and abound; and that this place may be a house of prayer for all time to come, to the glory and praise of the great name of our blessed Lord and Savior, Jesus Christ, who with the Father and the Holy Spirit, liveth and reigneth, ever One God, world without end. Amen.

The service concluded with the people joining in the recitation of the Nicene Creed.

Soon after the laying of the corner stone, work began on Christ Cathedral. The choice of an architect was one aspect with which Mrs. Batterson wanted to be involved. In a letter to Bishop Griswold, dated Holy Tuesday of 1904, she wrote:

Your letter reached me last evening, and I need not tell you how glad I am that you have secured the lot you wish. The question of an architect is one in which I have deep interest. Mr. Charles Burns of Philadelphia was a warm friend of my late hus-

band and one whose work as an architect was especially appreciated by him. He has built many churches which have been highly commended. He is an earnest churchman and I should like to have him consulted about the proposed church.

Mr. Burns was in fact hired for the Cathedral, along with Mr. Harry A. Macomb. Early on they provided various descriptions of the building. Included were details of construction materials, various measurements of the structure and plans for the organ. Special consideration was given to the system of support for the roofs; the transepts and choir were said to be formed with principal rafters and purlins, ceiled under jack rafters with narrow boards and moldings to form panels. The roof is slate, underlined with copper. The porch area consists of rafters showing below the ceiling but in the aisles the ceiling will be below the rafters, covered with ribs and moldings. According to plan, the choir floor was tiled, but all other floors were to be paved with cement.

The District of Salina Watchman, newsletter for the missionary district, reported more of the architects' ideas in their July 1906 issue:

The building will be heated by steam and lighted by electricity, the incandescent lamps being arranged behind the arches and rafters and against the walls back of the congregation, so that the light will be thrown toward the altar and will not inconvenience those looking in that direction... The stone facing is a beautiful soft creamy white color, showing natural split or 'pitched' faces without tooling, while the sills, arches and other cut stone work are of a slightly gray tone and finely dressed.

The Opening of the Cathedral

On January 8, 1908, Christ Cathedral opened her doors. The Salina Evening Journal recorded the happenings:

The event which has been looked forward to for several months took place today when the new Christ Cathedral was formally opened. The people of Salina as well as the members of the Episcopal Church have watched the progress of the building of the church with unlimited interest, knowing that it would be one of the finest buildings in the town, and a source of pride as long as the heavy stone structure would remain upon its foundation."

A note to Bishop Griswold from the Cathedral's architect, 1907.

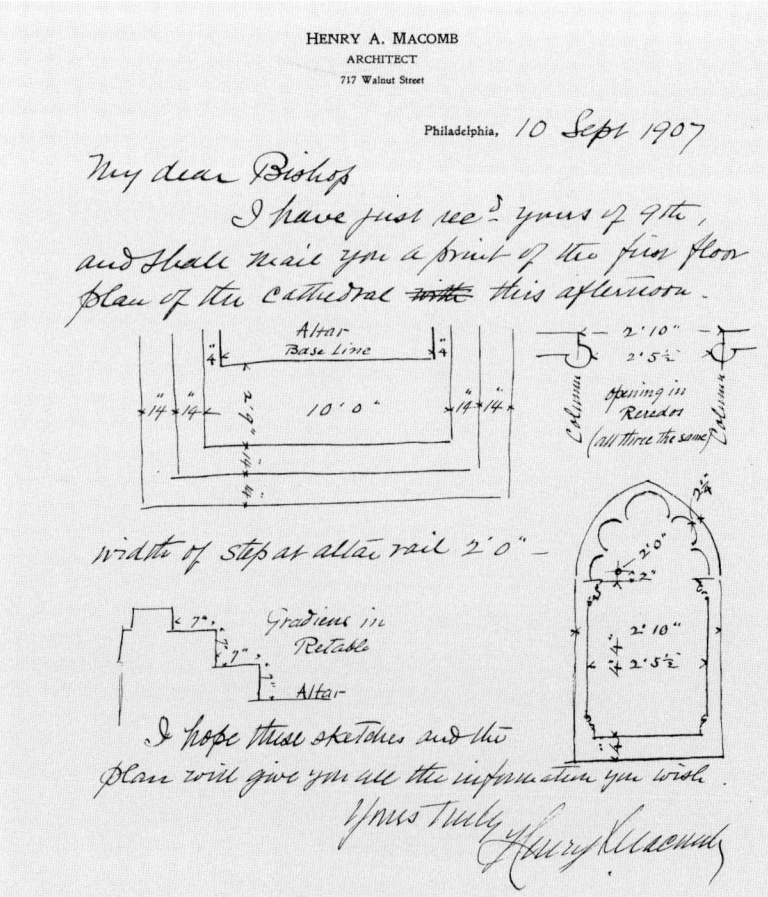

Present at the first service was Bishop Griswold, the dean, The Very Reverend William Masker, The Reverend Canon George Belsey and The Reverend G.B. Kinkead.

Bishop Griswold preached on the occasion; from the pulpit he exhorted the faithful saying:

From today forth — God willing — there never shall be a day when the Holy Eucharist is not celebrated in this building, no day without the holy worship ordained by God himself. In a Church for all the people it is to be expected that worship shall be rendered with as much dignity as possible, and yet with simplicity, and this will be our aim in the service here. Here also, all who care to do so can find all the privileges of the Catholic Church, all its means of grace, all the Sacraments — not two Sacraments only, but all the Sacraments.

Many clergy from the area also made the trek to Salina for the grand opening along with people from around the region who had watched with interest as the Cathedral was constructed. A special feature of the liturgy was the music; Miss Grace Wellington led the choir and Miss Katherine Eberhardt played the organ. Stringed instruments were also present to accompany the musical numbers, which included the "Te Deum" and "God So Loved the World".

As music was an important feature at the first service in Christ Cathedral, so was it also at the consecration of the building on Ascension Day of 1908. Mr. Roland Diggle from St. John's Church, Wichita played the dedication recital that evening which brought the dedication festivities to a conclusion. The consecration liturgy itself included a sermon, preached by Bishop Frank Millspaugh of Kansas. In his address he commended the congregation to faithfulness: "Beloved, [it is worship that] has been striven for in the building of this beautiful and substantial church, precious memorial of a faithful parish priest. May you all in God's good time realize its power for good!"

IV. Behind the Red Doors

Behold, heaven and the highest heaven cannot contain thee; how much less this house which I have built! Yet have regard to the prayer of thy servant and to his supplication, O LORD my God, hearkening to the cry and to the prayer which thy servant prays before thee this day; that thy eyes may be open night and day toward this house, the place of which thou hast said, 'My name shall be there,' that thou mayest hearken to the prayer which thy servant offers toward this place. And hearken thou to the supplication of thy servant and of thy people Israel, when they pray toward this place; yea, hear thou in heaven thy dwelling place; and when thou hearest, forgive.
— *1 Kings 8:27-30*

THE BUILDING

In the First Book of The Kings, one reads of King Solomon building and adorning the Temple of the Lord. While Kansas has had no king, Solomon did have twentieth century contemporaries who labored and offered treasures to God at Christ Cathedral. Building a church is obviously no small task; not only must the exterior be solid, but inside the furnishings have to be complete, down to the smallest linen in the sacristy. The talents and generosity of many people, from all over the globe, were used in Salina for decorating and supplying the new cathedral.

The cathedral was designed on the pattern of an Early English Gothic church, just the way Bishop Griswold wanted it. The structure with a medieval flare was figured with all native Kansas stone: the facing pieces came from Cottonwood Falls, Kansas, and the dressed stone from Silverdale, Kansas. The door sills and steps came from Lyons County. The design is simple and unpretentious, with very little molded work and no stone carvings.

Inside the cathedral, the medieval style of architecture is also present. The cruciform (or cross) shaped building stems from the early days of Christian buildings. Christ Cathedral's plan includes a choir, nave, transepts and choir aisles. At the crossing is a great tower, supported by four arches. The extreme length of the building is 119 feet and the width across the transepts is seventy-one feet. The height is roughly equivalent to a six-story building. The high altar is of Carthage marble with a reredos of Silverdale stone and it is behind the altar one will find the memorial inscribed to Father Batterson.

The Cathedral's Rood Beam, a memorial gift to Mrs. Batterson from Bishop Griswold, as it appeared Easter, 1991.

Among the finest features inside Christ Cathedral are the figures on the rood screen. The entire Rood was the gift of Bishop Griswold in memory of Mrs. Batterson in 1918. The Crucified Lord, with the Blessed Virgin and the Beloved Disciple was carved by a relative of the Lang family, working for a firm in Fond du Lac, Wisconsin. The Langs immigrated to the United States from Oberammergau, Germany, after being ostracized by their fellow countrymen. It seems that one of the sons took on the role of Judas in the town's famous Passion Play but after the production was complete, the locals would no longer buy from the Langs. The Bishop of Fond du Lac, The Right Reverend Charles Chapman Grafton, arranged their employment in America.

The baptismal font which sits in the south transept was the one font from Christ Church. It was carried across the street and first placed in the Blessed Sacrament Chapel. The lectern and pulpit are magnificently carved oak pieces. The lectern is a double one, with stands for two Bibles which swing around on a pivot. It was given in memory of Bishop Vail, the first bishop of Kansas. The pulpit, which sits opposite the lectern at the edge of the crossing, on the north side was built to accommodate four statues. At the time of the first service only the carving of Saint Paul had been completed. The pulpit was given as a memorial to The Right Reverend Elisha Smith Thomas, the second bishop of Kansas and founder of Saint John's Military School.

The Salina Evening Journal for May 22, 1953 reported the placement of three additional carvings in the pulpit, Saint Peter, Saint John and Philips Brooks. This later work was done by by Lester Raymer, an artist from Lindsborg, Kansas, a town to the south of Salina. The carvings of the apostles were given by Mrs. Leonard Hammond in memory of her husband and mother. The statue of The Right Reverend Philips Brooks (a famous preacher, one time bishop of Massachusetts and a man who himself probably disapproved of statuary in Episcopal churches) was given by Henry A. Pickering, long time sexton of the Cathedral. The Very Reverend Frederic W. Litchman, Dean in 1953, said "It is a particularly appropriate memorial for Mr. Pickering, inasmuch as they were contemporaries."

The rail at the high altar is black oak, supported by iron standards. It was a gift of the men of the parish in memory of Bishop Frank Millspaugh, the third bishop of Kansas. It was during his episcopate the Missionary District of Salina was created. The Prayer books and hymnals were donated by the New York Bible and Prayer Book Society. The initial set of vestments for the Cathedral came from donors in New York and Philadelphia. Deaconess Frances Kennett of Salina made burses and veils for the chalice and paten. The altar cross, candles and many of the other original furnishings were gifts by friends of Bishop Griswold from Hudson, New York, and other East coast cities.

Only 160 chairs were in place for the opening day; 300 others were delayed. Like much of the rest of the furniture, the chairs were hand carved, black oak, with wicker seats and a kneeler attached for use by the person in the row behind. Proper cathedral chairs, in lieu of the usual pews, was another wish of Sarah Batterson for Christ Cathedral. The chairs were all purchased from the Manitowoc Seating Works in Wisconsin. Over the years, extensive repairs and maintenance have been done on the chairs, so that many remain usable to this day. Retired Salina doctor, Neal Jenkins has now taken on their upkeep as a labor of love.

The furniture in the choir is complete to the last detail. Twenty of the stalls were set aside for clergy, fourteen of which are beneath an exquisitely hand carved canopy. Cathedral churches normally have room for extra clergy, as the cathedral is the mother church for the diocese and a center for worship. (Medieval tradition states that every cathedral should have ten resident canons, each with a specified responsibility annexed to his stall, for the word "dean" in Latin comes from word for the number ten.) The dean himself has a special stall; in Christ Cathedral it is on the north side behind the lectern. The wooden fixture, complete with canopy was a gift of parishioners of Dean Masker from his previous cure in Springfield Center, New York. The

ALL HAIL THE POWER OF JESUS' NAME   23

Christ Cathedral's Nave and High Altar.

inscription reads "Blessed is the man whose strength in in Thee, in whose heart are the highways of heaven."

Toward the back of the choir, and opposite the dean's stall is the bishop's throne, the singular item which sets a cathedral apart from a parish church. The word "cathedra" literally means "seat" and it is from this place that a bishop presides over his flock. The Cathedral throne is carved in the same style as the other stalls, but is elevated about twelve inches and stands almost ten feet tall. A bishop's mitre forms the canopy over the seat and a hand carved seal of the bishop is cut in the dark wood in the back of the seat. The throne is an original piece in the Cathedral, donated by a personal friend of Bishop Griswold. The throne bears the inscription, "The gift of a friend of the first bishop of Salina". Needlepoint cushions, (along with kneelers for the high altar rail,) were woven during the time of Dean Litchman to replace the original upholstered Spanish leather.

The Cathedral was well-maintained for a number of years and when the men were called off to war, the women and children in the parish took over the tasks of cleaning and repairing. However, many years of wear took their toll and in late 1976 the Dean and Vestry launched a campaign of over $100,000 to fix the plant and put in a new organ. The Very Reverend Sylvan Law, then Dean, wrote in the restoration brochure, "We stand at a crucial point in the history of Christ Cathedral. The past record of witness and service to this community by our parish is good. However, if we are to continue and to expand this record, it is necessary for us to be good stewards of the facilities that we have inherited from previous generations. I hope and pray that you will respond generously to the 'Cathedral Restoration Campaign'." The campaign dinner at the Salina Hilton to kick off the project featured the Dean of St. Matthew's Cathedral, Dallas, as speaker. One of the major problems to correct was water damage to the stone, caused by repeated freezing and thawing. The money was collected and the buildings restored.

The Nave Altar

For over eighty years the main area of focus in Christ Cathedral was appropriately the high altar. Under The Very Rev'd M. Richard Hatfield, the thirteenth dean, though, a free standing altar was placed in the nave. Since the 1960's (the era of Vatican II in the Roman Church and liturgical renewal within the Anglican communion,) a

Construction of the pace for the Nave Altar, 1990.

move was begun to bring altars closer to the people. For years, the Church correctly taught a transcendent and mystical approach to the Mass and this idea was best conveyed by a priest with his back to the people. However, an equally valid theology, which dates to the early days of the Church, is that the Eucharist is a thanksgiving feast in which the whole community participates. That means the priest has to assume a position facing the people, like a father at the head of the table. The move to a nave altar has also served a valuable utilitarian purpose in that those seated in the transepts are able to see the altar.

With a bit of grumbling, some misunderstandings and lots of teaching, the altar from St. Mary's Chapel was moved to the nave in June, 1990 and placed on an elevated platform, extending from the east end of the choir. A Jacobean frontal, in the "coronation pattern" was given and the move gradually won acceptance. The platform was enlarged a year later and dedicated in honor of Mrs. Helen Litchman. Daily Mass has been celebrated from this altar since the move. The high altar meanwhile, took on a new dignity when the blessed sacrament was moved there; a move which made it easily accessible to the clergy and at the same time provided new opportunities for devotion to the sacrament.

St. Mary's Chapel

It is customary around the world that cathedrals have a "Lady Chapel", an area dedicated to the Blessed Virgin. In large buildings, the chapel is often in an apse, the area behind the high altar. At Christ Cathedral, the St. Mary Chapel is in the north transept. It was dedicated by Bishop Griswold in January, 1911. It was initially furnished with items from the old Christ Church, including the original altar which was consecrated in 1887 in memory of Father Thomas Dooley, the first rector. Numerous faithful people have made gifts to the chapel, including Miss Margaret Utt who gave the statue of the Virgin and child in the 1940's.

In 1978 the area was renovated in memory of Katherine Davis Waddell to accommodate a free standing altar. Weekday Eucharists were then offered at this altar. In 1990, when the altar was moved to the nave to be used as the free standing altar, the altar from St. Peter's, Minneapolis, Kansas, which had been closed, was moved to the St. Mary Chapel and again placed against the wall. A year later the whole area was rededicated on the Feast of Saint Mary (August, 15) and included votive lights, a shrine candle and blue carpet.

The Blessed Sacrament Chapel / The Chapel of Saint Michael the Archangel

The Blessed Sacrament Chapel, located in the northwest corner of the cathedral was designed during the time of Dean Kinkead (1910-1917). The white marble altar came from a quarry in Marble, Colorado, where Kinkead had some financial interests. It was paid for over a period of several years by the children of the Cathedral with their Sunday School offerings. The tabernacle, fitted in the center of the altar was used for reserving the Sacrament until 1991. The cross on the altar came from the former church building; it was a memorial to Ellen Vail, given at Christmas 1895. An aumbry in the south wall of the chapel was later given as a receptacle for the holy oils.

The white marble altar in St. Michael's Chapel (formerly The Blessed Sacrament Chapel), dates from the time of Dean Kinkead.

Bishop Sheldon Griswold's personal crucifix, given to the Cathedral, hangs on the north wall of St. Michael's Chapel.

In 1957 an Honor Roll was erected on the south wall, listing the names of those who had served in World War II; stars were added to the names of those who died in conflict. One of the stained glass windows was also given in honor of Cathedral veterans. One of the most treasured pieces in the whole cathedral is the Chapel crucifix which belonged to Bishop Griswold and which he requested be sent to Salina, from Chicago, upon his death in 1931.

The Chapel began to take on a new look in 1982 when a columbarium was installed on the east wall of the chapel. This was done through a bequest of John Williamson, one time Senior Warden of the Cathedral. The columbarium was constructed so that marble slabs cover niches where the remains of the faithful are interred. Other gifts which followed, included pews given by Thomas Snyder; a chandelier given in thanksgiving by Mr. and Mrs. Leonard Wood; and carpeting given in thanksgiving by D.A. Norris (who contributed floor coverings in the rest of the building as well.)

The latest change in the chapel was a new name. What may seem like a bold move was actually quite logical: a locking tabernacle, a memorial gift, was placed in the high altar and so the sacrament was moved there from the Chapel. With the columbarium in place, the area had a new feel, and so it was thought appropriate to change its dedication. The best candidate was Saint Michael, patron of those of have died and the guardian and weigher of souls. Plus, with a stained glass window of the archangel already in place, it was an easy decision to change. An added reason for the new dedication was as a tribute to Dean Litchman, whose early formation was at St. Michael's Church in Marblehead, Massachusetts and whose remains lie in the columbarium.

The Choir Tiles

One of the loveliest features of the Cathedral is unfortunately one that many people never take the time to appreciate. That is the quarry tiles which decorate the floor of the choir. Cathedral architect, Harry Macomb, chose fourteen different designs from a potter at the Moravian Pottery and Tile Works in Doylestown, Pennsylvania; the cost was less than $800. Henry Mercer began his tile business at the turn of the century, inspired by the designs he encountered in medieval churches and castles in England and France. His catalogue from 1900 states that "builders of churches ... might welcome these heirlooms from the ecclesiastical floor of Castle Acre, Jervaulx and ... Cluny Abbey"

The patterns Macomb ordered for Christ Cathedral were chosen from an Early Gothic selection. Each of the two square-inch authentic decorative tiles are surrounded by larger, plain tiles. Included in the designs are the Star of David, a symbol associated with Judaism; grapes, the traditional symbol for wine; the Maltese Cross, adopted by the Knights of Malta, an association of philanthropists; dolphins, an early Christian symbol for the resurrection and salvation; ships, which are images of the Church; there are also quatrefoils based on those at Jervaulx Abbey in Yorkshire, England; wheels and dragons like those at Castle Acre in Norfolk, England; and the swastika of Persepolis, an ancient religious symbol dating to 4000 B.C. The sanctuary at the high altar is paved with unglazed Moravian tiles, and a mosaic design of stripes, castles, little chequers and fleur de lys from the Hotel de Cluny in Paris. The borders in both parts of the chancel are laid with three inch, French triangles.

The Stained Glass Windows

No one can step inside Christ Cathedral without feeling a sense of awe at the beauty of the stained glass. People of all faiths throughout Salina admit that no finer glass exists within the city, and probably within the entire region. The stained glass in the cathedral has been installed in stages — from the very beginning, up through and continuing to the present day. The student of stained glass knows that new and special features of the various window can be uncovered by looking at them from

Detail of floor tile in chancel of Cathedral.

Repairs had to be made to the Ascension window at the Cathedral, 1991.

different angles, at different times of the day and under different sky conditions. Longtime admirers of the windows will also explain how the stained glass can "come alive" during worship and prayer.

The first window ever placed in the Cathedral was the Archangel Uriel, placed in the north wall of the chancel in 1909. It was a gift in memory of Mrs. Alfred Claflin, who, in 1907, gave the Cathedral chimes in memory of her husband. It was purchased from the Gorham Company of New York, which at the time designed a complete plan for stained glass, calling for the best England could provide.

Four of the most notable windows are those found at the four compass points — the Ascension window in the east, the archangels in the west, the Baptismal window on the north and the Last Supper window to the south. The Ascension window which rises above the main entrance depicts Our Lord and two angels ascending above eleven colorfully clothed disciples. The prominence of this window is very appropriate since the Cathedral's annual Feast of Dedication is always Ascension Day, in recognition of the day the Cathedral was consecrated in 1908. The window was made by the Lamb Studios and given by the congregation as a whole in 1961. However, it had to be sent back because the nail holes were missing from the hands and feet of Christ, thereby not conforming to Scripture. The window had to be repaired in the Fall of 1991 when it began to collapse. Repairmen were brought in from the east coast to reinforce the window and prevent it from folding up like an accordion. The corrections were made just in time for the Cathedral to host the Diocesan Convention that year.

Opposite the Ascension window, in the liturgical East end of the building, which happens to be the West, geographically, are five windows titled "The Worship of Heaven". This series of windows installed between 1912 and 1925 consists of Christ the King surrounded by four archangels; [left to right,] St. Raphael, "the health of God"; St. Michael, "the strength of God"; St. Gabriel, "the messenger of God"; and St. Uriel, "the light of God". The three center windows were put in place for Christmas Eve 1912, given by the whole parish. The two outside windows were purchased with funds raised by the women of the Cathedral who prepared and served meals to the Lion's Club each week for a period of thirteen years. All five panels were made by the Black, Starr, Gorham

Company of New York and placed above the high altar to reflect the phrase at Mass which precedes the Sanctus — "Therefore, we praise you, joining our voices with angels and archangels and all the company of Heaven ..."

The window of the Last Supper standing above the doors of the South Transept is the Cathedral's lone piece of English glass. In fact, just the one piece made it to the Cathedral before the outbreak of World War I at which time it was decided it was unsafe to ship glass to America. The company contracted to make the window was the famous Kempe Studio in London. Part of the story of the company is contained in a letter written to one of this book's original researchers by Mrs. Margaret Stavridi, daughter of the artist at Kempe, who undertook a history of the firm in 1979.

The Kempe Studio was started by Charles E. Kempe in London, in a small way in 1868, with a glass works added in 1874. It differed from other stained glass firms in that Kempe was a dedicated Christian of High Anglican Church persuasion and looked upon his work as a vocation, and the decoration of a church as an act of homage. A severe speech impediment had prevented him from becoming a clergyman. He was a man of immense knowledge and of great taste, but was not a professional artist or draftsman. John W. Lisle served as his artist and continued with the company as art director after Kempe's death. He died himself, in 1927; the company closed down in 1934.

During the sixty years of its existence, Kempe's produced 4700 stained glass windows; 328 in America. The Last Supper Window of Christ Cathedral is well documented with all the specifications of shape, size, positions and subject in an order book of the C.E. Kempe & Company, now stored in the Art Archives of the Victoria and Albert Museum, London. Against the diagram sketch of the window is the word 'new', which means that the glass was specially designed by my father (John W. Lisle) and was not made from a previous cartoon. To complete its authenticity, there is a fine black and white photograph in the album of my father's work.

The window was made in a fifteenth century Flemish style, using an antique white-glass which is lighter in color than the windows of a later period. The main scene is the twelve apostles seated around the table with Jesus for Passover. A sanctuary lamp symbolizes the presence of Christ in the Sacrament. A knife lying on the table with its handle near Judas (who has no halo) and which is pointed toward Jesus signals the betrayer and his victim. A jar of red flowers on the floor next to Judas is an additional indication of the bloodshed to come. By contrast there is a jar of white lilies next to one of the disciples, prefiguring the Resurrection. The window was given by Dean Kinkead in memory of his parents.

One of the favorite windows for many people is the Baptismal window which stretches above the north doors. This window showing the baptism of Christ is full of symbols pertaining to Christian initiation. The depictions include a dove, the Holy Spirit, who descended upon Jesus at his baptism, and rays which represent the voice of the Father who said "This is my beloved Son..." To the left of St. John the Baptist are locust trees and bees, his symbols; and to the right of Jesus is an angel holding his mantle. Above and below the main picture are other symbols associated with water and redemption: there is an eagle diving into the lake after its eyes have been burned in the sun — symbolic of redemption by baptism; three fish which stand for all those commissioned by Christ to go and baptize in the name of the Trinity. Along the bottom of the panel is a depiction of Noah and the seven souls saved from the Flood; stags drinking from the water of life as recorded in Psalm 42; an eagle holding a fish, a medieval representation of the redeemed being taken to Heaven; and a water lily which symbolizes not only baptism, but purification. This window was given for Bishop and Mrs. Robert Mize (1921-1938) by their sons. The Reverend Robert H. Mize, Jr. ("Father Bob") dedicated the window in November, 1958.

There are many other gorgeous and interesting stained glass windows in the Cathedral, given by a variety of generous and loving clergy, parishioners and friends. Among the other windows of note, is The Crucifixion, found on the south side of the choir, given in memory of the Lee family, turn of the century merchants in Salina, and founders of the Lee Jean Company. Other distinguished windows include The Rising of Lazarus on the south wall of the nave and The Resurrection, on the north side of the chancel. In the narthex are a series of windows of Christ which use the Beatitudes and "I am" sayings as a theme. In the St. Michael Chapel are a collection of memorial windows, including one given in memory of Deaconess Gilliland who worked with poor children at St. Faith's House. Also in the Chapel is a memorial window for the clergy, one for war veterans, and of course, a panel of the patron, St. Michael.

Among the newer windows are those in the Choir Room on the south side of the Cathedral. In this collection is the Nativity Scene, a photographic gem. Just off the choir room, in the ladies room is St. Clare washing the lepers. Fr. Hatfield has said "We're probably the only church in Christendom with such a lovely stained glass window in our restroom." The Acolyte Room in the southwest corner of the building is the location for any new pieces of stained glass. Currently, there is a single window showing Fr. Charles Lowder, an English priest and founder of a priest's fellowship, (The Society of the Holy Cross, SSC), along with Fr. James DeKoven, a founder of Nashotah House, and the Nashotah House seal. The next windows to be dedicated are one showing Bishop Charles Grafton, Bishop of Fond du Lac, Wisconsin and "coach" of Bishop Griswold, along with Sister Agatha of the Sisters of the Holy Nativity who ministered in western Kansas around the turn of the century. The other is of Edward Pusey and John Keble, key figures in the Oxford Movement, begun in England in 1833.

Music: The organ and bells

Whether one is a regular at Sunday Mass, attends an occasional Evensong, or happens into the cathedral for a wedding or funeral, none can leave without the knowledge that Christ Cathedral has one of the finest musical instruments around. A cathedral organ should of course, be nothing short of the finest. The classical pipe organ at Christ Cathedral was built by the M.P. Moller Company of Hagerstown, Maryland. It was installed in 1977 in conjunction with a Cathedral restoration program. A dedication concert was played by

The Trompette-en-chamade (the horizontal pipes) are one outstanding feature of the Cathedral organ, installed in 1977.

Cathedral organist Royce Young and the premier recital by the world renowned Diane Bish. The Moller replaced the original Cathedral organ which was installed in 1907 by the House of Pilcher, organ builders who had worked out of St. Louis since the early 1800's. It was a three manual instrument with pedals, a gift of Sarah Batterson.

The specifications for the new Moller organ include four divisions in the great choir area with the swell division which is under controlled expression and a console that is movable for concerts. The pipes range in size from less than one foot to thirty two feet. The pipes are constructed of wood, tin, lead and zinc. Crowning the pipe organ is the trompette-en-chamade, the rank of pipes which extend horizontally from the organ chamber. The organ as is sits presently is only partially complete, the original plan calls for an additional division of pipes.

The organ isn't the only musical feature of the cathedral; neighbors near and far will testify to the powerful presence of tower bells. The Cathedral tower bells have been heard throughout the community for over 80 years. The bells have rung for numerous occasions, including formal recitals, weddings, funerals and recently to celebrate the release of a prisoner held for years in the mideast. The bells ring daily, calling the faithful to prayer for the "Angelus" or "Regina Caeli". Christ Cathedral has the most complete carillon in the state. Other bells which ring in the city of Salina are merely recordings played through speakers.

The Cathedral bell's total weight is 10,280 pounds – the range is from 130 pounds to over a ton. Musically, the bells cover one and a half octaves. Access to the bells is by a narrow winding staircase in the South transept. The first eleven chimes, which cost $5000,

The tower bells at Christ Cathedral.

were installed in the bell tower in 1907, during the construction of the building. They were given by Mrs. Arthur Claflin in memory of her husband. The story goes that a team of horses with a rope and pulley were used to hoist the bells into place. The bells were cast by the Meneely Company of West Troy, New York, an offshoot of Paul Revere's foundry. After the bells had been placed, an inauguration concert was held with a team of bell ringers pulling on ropes. On Easter Day and the Monday and Tuesday following, changes were played along with music of the season and popular secular tunes.

Three more bells and a new keyboard with a timer were added in 1990, a gift by Mrs. Edgar Laubengayer in memory of her husband. These bells were cast by the Fristen Bell Foundry, the Royal Bell Founder and Aarle-Rixtel of Holland. Technological advancements made the horse team obsolete and so the new bells were lowered in to place with a crane. There is still place for nine additional bells, all on the higher end of the scale — their weight ranges from eighty to almost 600 pounds. The cost at 1992 prices for the whole collection is in excess of $50,000, ten times the cost of the original eleven.

There are two traditions concerning church bells which have been followed at Christ Cathedral; one is that they all be blessed by a bishop and secondly that they be named, (the new bells are "Faith", Hope" and "Charity".)

Bell #	Inscription	Weight
1	O Praise God In His Holiness	2,285
2	Praise Him In the Firmament of His Power	1,828
3	Praise Him In His Noble Acts	1,240
4	Praise Him According To His Excellent Greatness	997
5	Praise Him In the Sound of His Trumpet	840
6	Praise Him Upon the Lute and Harp	713
7	Praise Him In the Cymbals and Dances	532
8	Praise Him Upon the Strings and Pipe	442
9	Praise Him Upon the Well-tuned Cymbals	352
10	Praise Him Upon the Loud Cymbals	347
11	Let Everything That Hath Breath Praise the Lord	244
12	Hallelujah! Sing to the Lord a New Song ...	176
13	Hallelujah! Praise the Lord from the Heavens ...	154
14	Hallelujah! How Good It Is to Sing Praises ...	130
*15	Hallelujah! Praise the Lord, O My Soul	583
*16	I Will Exalt You, O God my King ...	253
*17	Blessed Be the Lord My Rock! ...	198
*18	Lord Hear My Prayer ...	141
*19	I Cry To the Lord With My Voice	119
*20	O Lord, I Call to You; Come to Me Quickly ...	108
*21	Deliver Me, O Lord, From Evildoers ...	99
*22	Lord, You Have Searched Me Out ...	90
*23	I Will Give Thanks to You O Lord ...	81

*Not yet purchased

The original Cathedral bells are inscribed with phrases of Psalm 150. The new bells and any additional bells will likewise be inscribed with verses from other joyful Psalms.

The Rest of the Physical Plant

When one speaks of the Cathedral, they often mean more than just the four walls surrounding the worship space. The word "cathedral" can be used in reference to the community of the faithful and it can also be used generically in reference to all the buildings and grounds. Over the years this latter definition has been used to include three deaneries, two parish halls and an education building.

The first rectory actually fell under the control of Christ Church. It was built in 1886 during the time of The Reverend Joseph Antrim. It was sold however, when funds were being raised to purchase lots for the present cathedral. The second rectory, an 1870's edifice, was just south of the cathedral, where the Parish Hall now stands. It was actually a small hotel, built by Mr. Underwood. At some point it was sold to Mr. Maxey who added a north wing. It was known as both the Maxey House and the Wittman House. In 1905, Sarah Batterson bought it with the intention of using part of it as a home for the dean and the added wing as a guild hall.

The first floor of the hotel had a well-equipped kitchen and a large social room which was used for dinners, parties, dances and various forms of recreation and entertainment. The second floor, arranged hotel fashion with rooms on either side, was used for Sunday School and at times as residence quarters. The Women's Auxiliary served dinner to the Lion's Club in the old hotel, as

Originally a hotel, Wittman House became the first deanery and guild hall.

well as holding bazaars and other money-making projects. There are accounts of pageants and minstrel shows. One activity was a club called "King Arthur's Court" which brought together young people from all parts of the city.

The complex became increasingly difficult to maintain and so the the guild hall was closed in 1936. It was reopened in 1937 for Convocation, but closed again in 1940. The loss of Sunday School space was a real set-back to the educational goals of the Cathedral. In 1942 both parts of the building were demolished. A year later the Cathedral purchased the house at 150 South Eighth to be used as a deanery at a cost of $8000, which was paid for by the parish. It served as the Deanery into the 1970's and next door to it, to the south, was a grand home, used as the bishop's residence. The latter has since been torn down, and the old Deanery, now Diocesan property, after being used for a while by Pathfinder's, has become Ashby House, a transitional shelter for homeless families.

When the Wittman House was razed it opened space for a proper guild hall (parish house). As soon as 1944, Dean James Golder wrote in *The Watchman* (the Missionary District's paper, which he also edited,) that the "Chief topic of discussion in Cathedral circles is the new Parish House which has for many years been prominent in the prayers of the congregation." The vestry approved a set of drawings and hired an architect to give specifications. A fund was begun by Mrs. Henry Putnam, in memory of her husband, to pay for the project. Four years later, the plans became a reality and building was begun.

In May, 1948, Cathedral Treasurer G.N. Waddell, wrote to one of the contractors relaying the following: "Things are progressing very well with the Parish House and it looks as if the building should be well completed sometime next month. At the present time they are putting on the trimming and finishing up the plumbing. We are ready to decide on light fixtures." That same month the vestry decided to borrow $2000 from a local bank to make up for unpaid pledges. The total cost of the project was just under $50,000. Later that year the building was ready to be used. Space included a large assembly room with a stage, a fireplace, a kitchen, restrooms, a library, and an upstairs apartment. The first occupants of the apartment were Mr. and Mrs. William Houser, he was given the title "Assistant to the Dean". The apartment was later used as a nursery and office for the Cathedral archivist. It has since housed the family of a dean waiting to buy their own home and is now used by the Canon-in-residence. At this writing, plans are under way to modernize the building, including the installation of air conditioning.

The last major building project to be undertaken was the building of the Sunday School complex, erected during the time of Dean Frederic Litchman. After an existing apartment building was removed, ground was broken in 1955 and the two-story building begun. It sits to the south of the cathedral and extends east from the Parish Hall. The cost of the building was $75,000. The general contractor on the site was Mr. Mel Jarvis. The vestry awarded separate contracts for electrical work, plumbing and heating to Padgett Electric Co., City Plumbing Co., and Gage Plumbing and Heating Co.

The education wing was completed in 1956 and coincided with the fiftieth anniversary of construction on the cathedral. The stone on the facade was selected to match the Parish hall. When it opened there were offices in the east end, twelve class rooms, a large social

Construction of the Parish House, 1948.

room, rest rooms and storage space. The Weekly Times (the Cathedral newsletter) for April 1, 1956 said:

> *It was a joy to be able to use the new Sunday School building for the first time last Sunday. We used 'make shift' furniture, since new furniture is only on order, and although some of it is already on its way to us, it may take a week or two to reach us...*
>
> *Financially we stand at $4015 toward the 1956 goal of $4500. At the present it looks very much as if we shall meet the goal, and may even surpass it. From our point of view, members of Christ Cathedral are to be highly commended for a job superbly done. True we are not through yet, but ultimate success seems assured. Your participation in this project is a source of real satisfaction to you. God bless you all.*

The building changed very little in the next thirty five years. The office area was air conditioned, the Boy Scouts, music office and rehearsal area moved into the basement, a nursery was established on the upper level, The Saint George Bookstore and Gift shop opened on the top level in 1992 and one Sunday School room was converted to a conference room. The main emphasis of the complex though, is still as a place for Christian education and formation.

It is quite easy to get carried away in discussions of bricks and mortar, and it is easy to take pride in such lovely, well-planned buildings; and that is fine. One need always remember though, the Church is more than just walls and a roof; it is the people that make a Church, and the Church itself is the Body of Christ. Future generations will undoubtedly need to make changes and improvements, perhaps expand or even rebuild; but the faithful must always hearken back to the ideals of Sarah Batterson and Bishop Griswold, in that, this Church is to be a place of worship.

Christ Cathedral

ALL HAIL THE POWER OF JESUS' NAME 35

The Baptism of Jesus, South Transept of the Cathedral, given in memory of Bishop and Mrs. Robert Mize Sr., 1958.

The first stained glass window in Christ Cathedral, The Archangel Uriel.

One of the newest windows, in the Acolyte Room, Fr. Charles Luge Lowder, Fr. James DeKoven and the Nashotah House seal.

ALL HAIL THE POWER OF JESUS' NAME   37

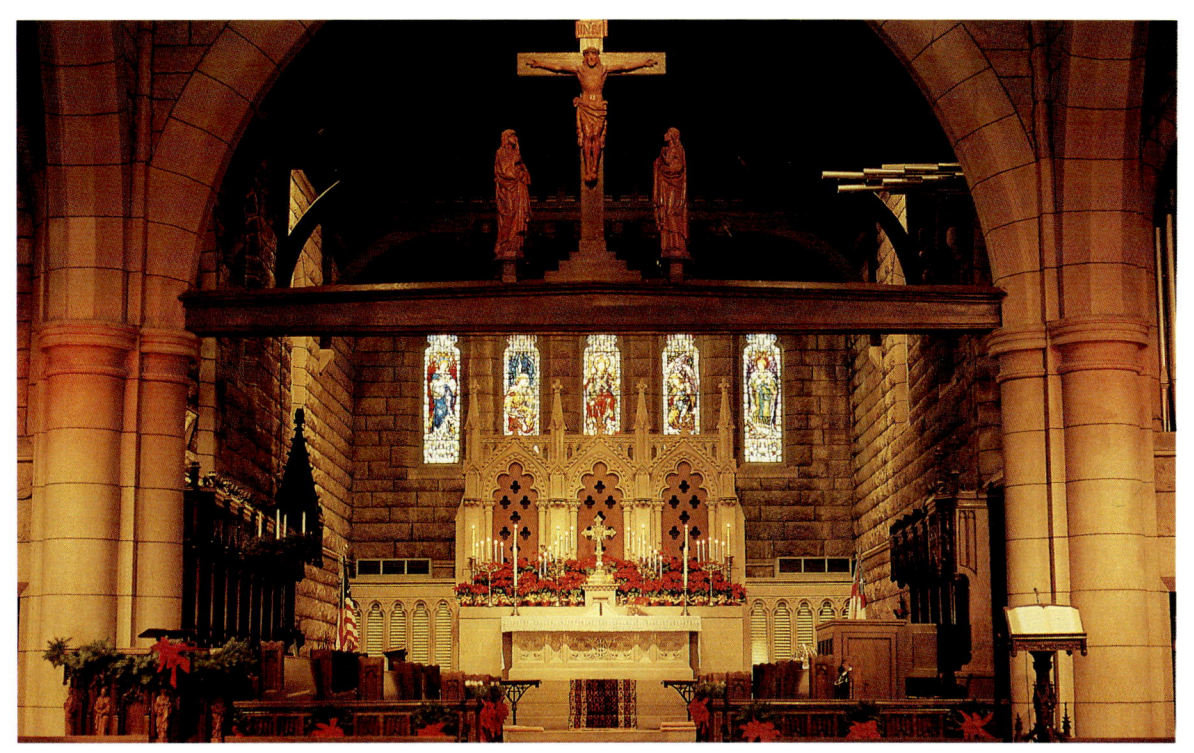

The Cathedral decorated for Christmas.

The Nativity Scene, given to the Cathedral in 1953.

The cast of the 1990 Christmas Pageant, Sunday School students of Christ Cathedral.

The Altar Party and Choir at the Feast of Lights Epiphany Celebration, 1991.

St. Elizabeth's Guild folds The Times, *1991; Clockwise from bottom left, Lukie Jarvis, Virginia Grosser, Lois Johnson, Ruth Thorp, Ruth Smith, Ruth Pelischek.*

Cathedral Youth Group at 1991 Diocesan Convention; left to right, Courtney Stockham, Kate Wood, Jennifer Favre, Deidre Hays, Kate Jacobus.

Jo Reed of St. Anne's Altar Guild, in the Cathedral sacristy.

Sara Osborn prepares a South African dinner, 1992.

The Nave Altar, constructed in 1990.

Barbara Young during construction of the Outdoor Stations.

42   All Hail the Power of Jesus' Name

Stained glass of Jesus, the Good Shepherd.

Dean Richard Hatfield at the Altar on Thnaksgiving Day.

V. Deans

For every high priest chosen from among men is appointed to act on behalf of men in relation to God, to offer gifts and sacrifices for sins. He can deal gently with the ignorant and wayward, since he himself is beset with weakness. Because of this he is bound to offer sacrifice for his own sins as well as for those of the people. And one does not take the honor upon himself, but he is called by God, just as Aaron was. So also Christ did not exalt himself to be made a high priest, but was appointed by him who said to him, "Thou art my Son, today I have begotten thee"; — Hebrews 5:1-5

WILLIAM RUSSELL McKIM
1901-1905

The last man to be called to Christ Church as rector, before the parish was designated as the cathedral, was The Reverend William Russell McKim. After completing studies at General Theological Seminary in New York, Fr. McKim was ordained priest and deacon in 1896. His first assignment was a large territory in Nebraska, where he served for four years. While there, his health failed and he took a year's absence from church work. In 1901 he accepted the call to Christ Church, Salina, where he made his home at 141 South Eighth Street.

At this time, Salina was a part of the Missionary District, which included the western two-thirds of the state of Kansas. The Right Reverend Sheldon M. Griswold had been consecrated Bishop of this area. Upon Griswold's arrival in Salina, in February of 1903, the young Fr. McKim was on hand to greet his new bishop at the train station.

By June, 1903, Christ Church had been organized into a Cathedral Chapter by Bishop Griswold. Father McKim was elected first Dean of the would-be cathedral. He led the vestry through the necessary ground work empowering Bishop Griswold to begin the process which would eventually result in the actual construction of a cathedral on the plains of Kansas.

In the spring of 1905, the Griswolds were host to a visitor from the east, a Miss Sarah E. Wheeler. A romance developed between Miss Wheeler and the bachelor priest, and that summer the smitten William McKim took an extended vacation to marry Sarah Wheeler at her home parish in Little Falls, New York. He was never to return to Salina, and so would never be seated in the Dean's stall at the cathedral.

While in New York, Fr. McKim received a call to St. John's Church, Oneida. He served there until 1919, when he moved to Rochester as rector to Trinity Church. Always plagued by health problems, he retired from that parish in 1934, and died in 1941.

✠

WILLIAM A. MASKER
1906-1911

During the five years that The Reverend William A. Masker served the newly-constructed Christ Cathedral, he became the first dean to occupy the Dean's stall. During his time, the Episcopal Church in Salina made a

The Very Reverend William Russell McKim. 1901-1905.

The Very Reverend William A. Masker. 1906-1911.

strong impact on the city of Salina and the whole region.

Masker was a graduate of Racine College in Wisconsin, and the General Theological Seminary in New York. He began his ordained ministry as a missionary in the Diocese of New York, then served as rector of Trinity Church, Athens, New York, for four years. Following that, he accepted a call to St. Mary's Church in Springfield Center, New York. It was from there that Bishop Sheldon Griswold called him to the Dean's stall at Christ Cathedral. He was described as a "man full of missionary spirit, enthusiastic energy and consecrated abilities." His wife, who was a native of Wisconsin herself, was thought to be "adaptable to the west."

The Cathedral Chapter confirmed Bishop Griswold's nominee by election. He was installed as Dean on February 11, 1906, and preached at the service. The following March, Bishop Griswold signed a contract with Cathbert and Sargent of Topeka for the construction of the stone cathedral building. The cost was

Preaching Service for Men Only
—At Christ Cathedral—
To Every Man in Salina, Come!
Sunday Afternoons At 4 O'clock Sharp
February 16
February 23
and March 1

Dean Masker offered this service for a specific audience, 1908-1909.

announced as $32,738, funded by Sarah Elizabeth Batterson. The Bishop broke ground for the new building on April 2, and on May 28, 1906, the Feast of the Ascension, the cornerstone was laid.

Dean Masker became involved in community projects and formed a Men's Club, later to become a chapter of the Brotherhood of St. Andrew. Members included early Salina names such as Watson, Heyward, Ober, Hiller, Winterbotham, Putnam, Brooks, Kimball, Quincy, Walker, Butzer and Crawford. By April, 1907, the Men's Club sponsored the first of a series of annual dinners, served by the ladies of the parish. At one such dinner in 1909, Bishop Griswold spoke of the need to sponsor a hospital for the city. The Men's Club was also instrumental in working on another project for the city — establishing Salina's first YMCA. The hospital and the YMCA projects were accomplished compatibly, owing much to the guidance of Bishop Griswold, supported by his Dean, William Masker.

Service to the youth of the parish started with the arrival of Deaconess Frances Kennett in October, 1906. Deaconess Kennett, originally from St. Louis, Missouri, had trained at the New York School for Deaconesses, and had spent ten years at Grace Parish in New York City. In 1904 she moved to Springfield, Illinois, and it was from there she came to Salina. She established a Sunday School program on the second floor of the guild hall.

Dean Masker instituted a children's service for Christmas Eve, 1910, followed by a Christmas party in the guild hall featuring a lighted Christmas tree. The boys' choir had made its first appearance the year before, with Kenneth Kastner, Harold Ess and Joseph Wilson among its members.

In January, 1911, Dean Masker submitted his resignation in order to accept a call as assistant dean for Christ Cathedral in St. Louis. Four years later, he moved to Washington D.C., where he was assistant at both St. Paul's and St. Mark's churches. In 1925, Dean Masker retired from parochial work and was employed as a librarian for the United States Coast and Geodetic Survey. He died in 1927.

In reporting the resignation of Dean Masker, Bishop Griswold cited several reasons to continue work without a dean. He assumed the work of the dean, assisted by Canon George B. Kinkead and Canon Lloyd Holsapple.

✠

GEORGE BLACKBURN KINKEAD
1911-1917

While in General Theological Seminary in New York, George Blackburn Kinkead (after graduation with a master's degree from Princeton University) was approached by the seminary dean to serve in the Missionary District of Kansas. Bishop Sheldon Griswold had petitioned the seminary with a plea for men to satisfy the need for priests in the distant regions of the District. Kinkead agreed to serve in Kansas for one year.

Kinkead was ordained deacon before coming to Kansas, and was a celibate member of the Order of the Holy Cross. Upon his arrival in Salina, he was met at the train station by the Reverend Robert H. Mize, headmaster of St. John's Military School, and three months later, in November, 1904, Bishop Griswold ordained Fr. Kinkead to the priesthood. He was then sent to serve St. Paul's Church in Beloit. In addition, he found-

The Very Reverend George B. Kinkead. 1911-1917.

ed a mission at Concordia and ministered to the needs of small congregations in Cawker City and Logan.

In 1909, the Bishop moved Fr. Kinkead to Salina and installed him as Canon Presenter of the Cathedral. He lived at the nearby YMCA, where The Reverend Lloyd Holsapple also resided. From December 1909 to September 1914, Fr. Kinkead edited the magazine for the Missionary District, entitled *The Watchman.*

Through this magazine, Kinkead published observations made on a world tour with the Secretary of the American Bible Society in 1906-1907. His articles included descriptions of the people of all classes he had encountered in his travels through Europe, Egypt, Burma, India and China.

In 1908, Fr. Kinkead accompanied Bishop Griswold to the Lambeth Conference in England. Both men returned to Salina eager to introduce a boys' choir to the Cathedral. The choir became a reality, and made its first appearance at Christmas, 1909.

When Dean Masker resigned in 1911, Bishop Griswold served as his own dean for several months, naming Fr. Holsapple as Canon Presenter and Canon Kinkead was given use of the deanery at 130 South Eighth Street, and a yearly salary of $720. He was thirty-two years old.

On September 17, 1911, Canon Kinkead was installed as the third Dean of Christ Cathedral. During this time he was assisted by Canon Holsapple and Canon H.P. Scratchley, curate, and The Reverend V.M. Beede. Deaconess Mabel Warner, who lived at the guild house, served as parish worker.

Dean Kinkead was described as indefatigable. For example, he conducted three services on Christmas Day, 1911, which were attended by nearly two hundred people. In his attempts to increase spiritual awareness, he focused on liturgy, music, regular weekday worship and study tracts, hoping to instill his congregation with this sense of missionary zeal.

Through the children of the parish, he introduced the Reserved Sacrament, using their Sunday School offering as a base for funding the Blessed Sacrament Chapel. He planned the Chapel as the place where the elements could be properly housed, there being no aumbry for the tabernacle on the high altar. He commissioned the white marble altar in the chapel, with a proper tabernacle made to house the Blessed Sacrament. Initially thought of as the "Children's Chapel", the first reference to communion from the Reserved Sacrament was noted on Palm Sunday, 1915. The Dean introduced a Children's Mass, which continued as a weekly service.

The entrance of the United States into World War I had profound effect on the young Dean. In June, 1916, a special service was held at the Cathedral, at which time the Colors were received from members of the Kansas National Guard leaving for military service overseas, to be held until their return. A Mass for the safety of the troops was begun and continued weekly on Wednesday mornings.

The financial situation at the Cathedral at this time began to weaken, and the Dean was not paid his full salary, which at this time had increased to $1500 per annum. The financial report of 1915 showed more than $200 in unpaid pledges, and an outstanding debt of nearly $675. The yearly budget of $5164 was dependent upon funds raised by the women's activities and donations from Bishop Griswold. The Bishop agreed to pay the insurance premiums for the Cathedral for four years, 1916-1920. In partial compensation for back salary owed to the Dean, the vestry agreed to purchase a garage for $150, which Dean Kinkead had built himself to house his newly-acquired automobile.

Dean Kinkead had artistic talents, and designed plans for the rood beam, which were accepted by the Cathedral Chapter in December, 1917. The design was presented to the Cathedral on behalf of Bishop Griswold, to be erected as a memorial for Mrs. Sarah Batterson, benefactress of the Cathedral, who had died in June, 1915.

Feeling a need to minister to the military troops involved in The Great War, Dean Kinkead announced his plans to resign, and preached his last sermon at the Cathedral on December 16, 1917. The congregation numbered 235 at this service, and seventy people attended his service of Evensong that Sunday. The popular Dean, with his Airedale dog, "Pemmy" (short for the Earl of Pembroke), left Salina the next morning. His fourteen years in Kansas had stretched far past the one year he had promised his seminary dean.

He sent his formal letter of resignation in January, 1918, and then enlisted in the U.S. Army as a chaplain. He served the troops at the front in Europe. Bishop Sage accepted his resignation and nominated him to the position of Honorary Canon, which the Cathedral Chapter endorsed unanimously.

On the last day of 1918, a petition was presented with sixty-six signatures to "ask, beg, and petition the Bishop and Chapter to extend a most earnest call to return to his parish our former Dean, Lieutenant George B. Kinkead." It would be a few more years before Fr. Kinkead would be paid his past due salary.

Following his discharge from the Army, Fr. Kinkead served in Corning, New York, until 1928, and then as chaplain for the College of Preachers for another ten years. He died June 14, 1955, after having retired from an active ministry in 1947.

✠

HENRY SEARS SIZER
1920-1921

The Reverend Henry Sears Sizer served an unique ministry at Christ Cathedral. During his tenure as Dean, the Missionary District of Kansas was without a Bishop, just as Christ Cathedral had been two years without a Dean.

A native of New York, Dean Sizer was graduated from the St. Andrew Divinity School in 1895, and from General Theological Seminary in 1898. He had been ordained deacon in 1895, and priest in 1898. Before coming to Salina, he had been at St. Jude's in Brooklyn.

Fr. Sizer was elected Dean in February of 1920, but did not begin his ministry in Salina until April 18 of that year. It was the second Sunday after Easter, and 320 were in attendance for the three services held by the new Dean that day. Two weeks earlier, Easter Day, April 4, the Service Register carried the notation, "Blizzard through the night. Snow 2 feet or more. What people came had to dig their own way through the snow." In spite of these conditions, sixty-two members made it to Easter services.

The Very Reverend Henry Sears Sizer. 1920-1921.

It was no surprise that in May the Church Property Committee made plans to provide adequate heating for the Cathedral. They hired the Salina Plumbing Company to do the work. This was a new business in town, and as a promotion had published a booklet advertising the advantages and convenience of indoor plumbing and heating. Pictured as examples in the booklet were the Bishop's residence at 154 South Eighth Street, as well as the property at 150 South Eighth Street which was later purchased for a Deanery.

Dean Sizer introduced Morning Prayer as the main service of worship during the summer months of July and August, and continued it on the first, third and fifth Sundays of each month thereafter. The Dean's installation took place on October 3, 1920.

In November, 1920, the Cathedral Chapter sent a telegram to the Reverend Robert H. Mize, urging him to accept his election as Bishop for the Missionary District, and pledging the support of the Chapter. Dean Sizer read the reply publicly on December 3, in which the Bishop-elect accepted his call and asked to be consecrated in the Cathedral. The ceremony eventually, however, was held in Topeka, January, 1921.

Apparently Dean Sizer saw the election of a new bishop as a signal for a new team, and submitted his resignation in the spring of 1921. It was accepted in June, and the Sizer family left Christ Cathedral in mid-July.

Dean Sizer returned to New York state and served as rector of the Church of the Evangelist in Oswego for many years. He died July 18, 1960, at the age of eighty-eight.

☩

FRANK VICTOR HOAG
1921-1929

Bishop Sheldon Griswold's influence was evident in the choice of fifth dean of Christ Cathedral. The Reverend Frank Victor Hoag was ordained priest by Bishop Griswold in January, 1917, shortly after the Bishop moved from Salina to the Diocese of Chicago. Griswold later recommended him to the post of Cathedral Dean.

Dean Hoag, born in 1891, graduated from the University of Wisconsin and Western Theological Seminary. After becoming a priest, he served as an Air Corps chaplain during World War I, and then as a parish priest in Geneva, Illinois, before coming to Salina as fifth dean of Christ Cathedral in September, 1921.

The Very Reverend Frank V. Hoag. 1921-1929.

His first endeavor was to hold a series of conferences with parishioners to outline a program for church work. Entitled "The People's Own Plan", the conferences were designed for all members to express their ideas and interests on the subjects of missions, social service, religious education and finance, in order to produce an overall annual plan for the parish. The area of religious education would be the Dean's focus while serving the people of the Cathedral.

In order to reach as many communicants as possible, the Cathedral installed a telephone service for shut-ins. Invented and designed by the local telephone company, the system (believed to be the first in the world) enabled up to ninety listeners to call the operator and be connected to one of two microphones in the Cathedral pulpit. Telephone records indicated that ninety listeners did indeed hear the first sermon preached by Bishop Robert H. Mize. An additional microphone was added later near the organ to improve the transmission of music. Choir soloists stood near a third microphone. Over the years, additional switchboard connections were added, eventually totalling 124.

Dean and Mrs. Hoag made their home at the rectory, 138 South Eighth Street, where, on January 21, 1922, a baby girl was born. Named Mary Faith, the baby died February 13. As a memorial to their first-born, the Hoags commissioned the construction of a small frame building on North Ninth Street, across from a public school, which was named

Dean Hoag visits St. Faith's House, named after his infant daughter.

St. Faith's House. The house was dedicated in October, 1922, and Eleanor Ridgway was placed in charge of the work there. Dean Hoag asked that the efforts of St. Faith's House serve as an out reach program for the welfare and religious education of all children, and he encouraged regular collections of money and materials to support the mission.

At the Cathedral itself, the Christian Nurture Series provided the basis of instruction for Sunday and weekday classes. Dean Hoag taught junior high school boys on Wednesdays. Senior high students met with him each Sunday evening for supper, social hour and an educational program, calling themselves the Ichthus Club.

The Dean sponsored children's pageants and plays, and the children's choirs. He took the Boy Scout Troop on hiking and camping trips, and worked to know each child personally.

Christmas Eve at four o'clock had become the traditional time for the boys' choir performance, usually with about 175 people in attendance. In 1925, Dean Hoag reintroduced the midnight service for Christmas Eve, which was overwhelmingly supported by nearly 290 communicants packed into the Cathedral.

During the school year 1922-1923, the Cathedral joined with other Salina churches in the "released time" program. Under this plan, the Salina School Board released children for a quarter day per week for religious instruction at the child's home church. Teachers recommended by the churches were appointed by the School Board as certified for instruction. This actually continued until 1935. On the national level, Dean Hoag served as secretary of the National Commission of Week-Day Religious Education from 1927 to 1932.

The great emphasis by Dean Hoag on religious education made a marked impact on attendance at public worship. An example can be seen in the numbers present at a 6:30 AM Easter Day service. In 1922, forty-three communicants were present, while in 1929, 105 made their communions. Attendance had doubled at the 11:00 service as well.

In the seven years that Dean and Jessie Hoag were in Salina, they acquired two children. In 1923, they adopted a son whom they named Sheldon Griswold after the Bishop, who had earlier ordained Dean Hoag and who recommended him for the position as Cathedral Dean. In 1927, the Hoag's daughter was born.

In July, 1929, the Hoag family left Salina for Eau Claire, Wisconsin, the Dean having accepted a call to serve as Dean of Christ Cathedral in that city. He stayed there until 1946.

In recognition of his work in the field of religious education, the Seabury-Western Theological Seminary in Chicago, conferred a Doctor of Divinity degree on Dean Hoag. He had served as editor of *Flashes in Religious Education*, the Province V magazine of the Episcopal Church, from 1935 to 1944. From 1944 to 1964 he wrote a regular column in *The Living Church*, called "Talks With Teachers."

From 1946 to 1950, The Reverend Dr. Victor Hoag served as associate rector of Trinity Church, Tulsa, Oklahoma, and he was a member of the Diocesan Board of Examining Chaplains. He continued to publish educational pieces, and later was named Executive Secretary of the Department of Religious Education for the Diocese of New Jersey.

Dean Hoag accepted a position as Director of Christian Education at the Chapel of Intercession in New York City, in 1955. He retired from that position in 1958, and moved to Florida, where he lived for another ten years.

✠

DONNON E. STRONG
1929-1933

Moving from Dean Hoag's emphasis on religious education, the sixth dean of Christ Cathedral, The Very Reverend Donnon E. Strong focused his ministry on spiritual and liturgical aspects of the Episcopal Church. This was appropriate, as the revised 1928 Book of Common Prayer was introduced during his tenure.

A graduate of General Theological Seminary, and a celibate Anglo-Catholic churchman, Dean Strong had been ordained a priest at twenty-eight years of age in June, 1924. He first served the Diocese of Western Missouri as rector of Christ Church, Warrensburg, and in his summers did supply work for the Anglican Church in Quebec, Canada.

A full schedule of services was maintained by Dean Strong, with a daily Eucharist at 7:30 AM. Confessions were available Saturday afternoons and by appointment. On Wednesdays, a breakfast was served in the guild house following Mass. On Fridays, the Dean offered an extra service for children at 4:15, and on Friday evenings, a Litany and sermon for everyone.

The 1928 Book of Common Prayer, introduced to the Cathedral congregation the first Sunday in December, 1929, was met with much disdain. Dean Strong announced in his newsletter that the revision had caused a "...furor on

The Very Reverend Donnon E. Strong. 1929-1933.

two continents. It shows the first (major) changes made in the service of this church in more than 300 years." In the United States, the 1928 book replaced the American version of 1892. Bishop Robert H. Mize commented that the most radical changes lay in "humanizing the prayer book."

In the fall of 1929, plans were completed to overhaul and rebuild the cathedral organ. The completion date was set for December 20, so that the organ would be in operation by Christmas, and the project was completed on schedule.

The men of the church provided Dean Strong with an automobile, presented to him in the fall of 1930. He said, "It is a joy to have one, and my gratitude is deeply felt." He added that he did not know how to drive one, and suggested parishioners give him a wide berth when they saw him behind the wheel.

In the summer of 1933, Dean Strong underwent surgery to remove his tonsils, which he thought might improve his declining health. However, after a church service on August 13, the Dean requested a leave of absence to spend a month or two in Evergreen, Colorado, where he thought the mountain air might speed his recuperation. During his time in Colorado, church services were maintained by Bishop Mize, with the assistance of The Reverend L. Mitchell.

In January, 1934, from a sanitarium in Denver for an "ailment of the lungs," Dean Strong sent his resignation to the Bishop. During the remaining few years of his life, he lived at The Oakes Home, an Episcopal establishment, and filled in occasionally at area churches.

Dean Strong died September, 1938, at the age of forty-two. At the same hour of his funeral and burial in Denver, Colorado, Bishop Mize celebrated a Requiem Mass at the Cathedral for its departed Dean.

✠

FREDRIC WILLIAM GOLDEN-HOWES
1934-1935

The Dean with the shortest tenure was number seven, Fredric William Golden-Howes, who arrived in November, 1934, and left July, 1935. Little information is available about him, except that he was born in England in 1886, and had previously served at Christ Church Cathedral in Mexico City, and had written several short stories in this Mexico setting.

In February, 1935, Dean and Mrs. Golden-Howes gave a tea in honor of Mr. H.A. Pickering's eighty-eighth birthday.

The Very Reverend Fredric W. Golden-Howes. 1934-1935.

Mr. Pickering was a long-time sexton at the Cathedral and beloved by the whole congregation. The Women's Guild presented Mr. Pickering with a check for $3.00 at its April meeting, a generous gift by the monetary standards of 1935. The gift was to express the appreciation of the Women's Guild to Mr. Pickering for the many services he rendered in his duties as sexton.

In the summer of 1935, Dean and Mrs. Golden-Howes left Salina so that he could substitute for a rector in New York City. He sent his resignation from there in August, and never returned to Salina.

Dean Golden-Howes died in Florida in 1961.

✠

HEWITT BRENAMAN VINNEDGE
1936-1941

Christ Cathedral's eighth dean, The Very Reverend Hewitt Brenaman Vinnedge, was a highly-educated man, with degrees from Miami University, the University of Chicago, and a doctorate from Marquette University. He spent the early Thirties as a professor at Drury College in Missouri; head of the history department at the State Teachers' College in Mayville, North Dakota; at Hastings College in Nebraska; and instructor in Latin and Greek at Nashotah House and was ordained a priest in 1932.

Vinnedge and his family arrived in Salina in March, 1936, following three years as rector of St. Alban's in McCook, Nebraska. He assumed a distressed financial situation at the Cathedral, a result of the Great Depression that had rocked the country a few years earlier. In his first sermon, Dean Vinnedge blamed the results of the Depression on a "lack of faith and separation of the world from God's word. Fiery serpents of unrest, near despair, and revolt would have found no foothold in the country had it practiced God's word."

The Dean announced a few weeks later, in his Easter Day sermon, that he felt the people of the Cathedral should be told frankly what the financial situation was. Pledges for 1936 amounted to less than $1500, and a floating debt alone amounted to about $1000. He requested that the congregation make an additional Easter offering to be applied to the outstanding debt "in the spirit of Lenten sacrifice." Three years later he would be able to announce that the debts had been removed and that the Cathedral's bills were currently being paid. At the Annual Meeting in 1940 he further reported that the mortgage had been reduced to $1800.

The Very Reverend Hewitt B. Vinnedge. 1936-1941.

In 1937, Dean Vinnedge presented a religious drama on the new KSAL radio station the first Sunday after its opening. Thereafter, he hosted a weekly radio program on the history of religion, entitled, "The Cathedral Hour." He also directed a broadcast of the Midnight Mass on Christmas Eve of that year.

Active in community affairs, the Dean granted the Salina Community Theater use of the guild hall twice a week. He served as chaplain for the Elks lodge, and was an active member of the Kiwanis Club. He gained a reputation as a public speaker and was often asked to address various groups and meetings. Among these was the Commencement address for Salina High School in 1938.

The Dean also filled posts in the Diocesan Council of Advice, the Board of Examining Chaplains, and was deputy to the General Convention of 1937.

Church membership figures rose during Dean Vinnedge's time at Christ Cathedral. and he reorganized the boys' choir. While the nucleus of the boys' choir consisted mainly of St. John's Military School cadets, it was open to any interested boy in the city.

Dean Vinnedge announced in November, 1941, that he planned to resign and return to teaching at Nashotah House. He taught New Testament there for the next six years, and also wrote poetry, prose and songs. He also served as literary editor of *The Living Church* from 1945 to 1947, and was book review editor for another publication, Parsons, for several years before his death in 1957.

After Nashotah House, Dean Vinnedge moved to another teaching position at Mississippi South College. Upon leaving there he served small parishes in Mississippi. His lasting devotion to Nashotah House, and an example of his writing, is evident in the following tribute:

"Nashotah"

Here may the eye behold a rich array of woodland beauty; tree and lakes, unkempt and virgin loveliness, and wild flowers gay and bright in spring — where none tries to preempt each foot of land for gain.

The very air is vibrant with the lingering poignancy of hopes and dreams and thanks poured forth in prayer and praise to God, throughout a century.

Here men have kept the faith, and offered up The Body of the Lord obediently;

Here in His sacrifice have given the cup of His Most Precious Blood.

Here may they see the vision of a life, yielded to bring more faithful subjects unto Christ their King.

✠

JAMES TOLMIE GOLDER
1941-1946

The first day of April, 1941, marked the arrival of two men who would guide and direct the District and the Cathedral for the next several years. They even lived next door to each other in their respective official residences. They were The Right Reverend Shirley Nichols, Bishop of the Missionary District of Kansas and The Very Reverend James T. Golder, Dean of Christ Cathedral.

As the ninth Dean of the Cathedral,

The Very Reverend James T. Golder. 1941-1946.

Father Golder had graduated from Ripon College, Northwestern University and Nashotah House. He was ordained deacon in 1932 and priested the following year. He served as a missionary at Spooner Shell Lake and Cumberland, Wisconsin, for three years, and then became the rector at St. Peter's Church, Ripon, Wisconsin, in 1936. He found the Wisconsin winters hard on his health, and welcomed the opportunity to move south to Kansas when he

Dean Golder and choir members line up outside the Cathedral, Easter, 1942.

received the call to Christ Cathedral.

His first order of business was to liquidate an old $1800 mortgage belonging to the Cathedral, and with his enthusiastic direction, the mortgage was paid off in five weeks. A few months later, Mr. Leonard Wood, a Vestry member, suggested Dean Golder's salary be increased $15 per month, raising his yearly wage to $2280. He was also to be given a $30 Christmas bonus.

Sale of some Salina property made possible a gift from Mrs. H.J. Putnam, which led to the construction of a new parish house. Mrs. Putnam provided additional funds which permitted the Dean to refurbish the Blessed Sacrament Chapel. Mrs. Golder made new dossals in liturgical colors for the openings behind the high altar. The chimes, which had been silent for several years, were reconditioned and played again regularly. The Dean's son, Jim, was one of the carillonneurs. Many other gifts, such as a new processional cross, a sterling silver chalice and paten, and Eucharistic vestments, were given to the Cathedral during Dean Golder's tenure.

At the Dean's request, Bishop Nichols authorized the gift of an Anglican Altar Missal in memory of Caroline Link Fischer, in 1943. It was for use in weekday services other than Holy Days provided for in The Book of Common Prayer. Reflecting traditional Nashotah House churchmanship, Dean Golder celebrated the Eucharist in a "high church" manner — smells and bells. Some members of the congregation preferred a less "Roman" practice, but the Dean had ample support for his style.

The large Sullivan house at 150 South Eighth Street, immediately north of the Bishop's residence, was purchased in 1943 for $6500 and renovated as the new Deanery. A year earlier, the guild house at 128 South Eighth had been removed, costing the Cathedral $451. Dean and Mrs. Golder hosted a breakfast at the Deanery on Youth Sunday, an event observed by members of the Griswold Club. It was also in 1943 that the Cathedral was incorporated with the State of Kansas as a charitable institution.

Dean Golder was much involved in community affairs, and in 1944 served as a member of the Saline County Ration

Board; a manager of the local U.S.O. for "Colored Troops"; as a member of the OCD Youth Commission; and on the Chamber of Commerce Committee on Colleges and Schools. He was also a member of the local Red Cross, and chaplain for the Elks lodge.

Within the District, Dean Golder was active on several committees and edited *The Watchman*, the district's newsletter. He was also vice-president of the Executive Board. Bishop Nichols had high regard for Dean Golder's quiet and informal ministry in the field of alcoholism through his membership in the Recovered Alcoholic Clergy Association. In the years following his work in Salina, Dean Golder served on a number of diocesan commissions on alcoholism, was elected president of RACA in 1968. In recognition of his work in this area, he received an honorary doctorate from Nashotah House in 1964.

Although he received several calls, Dean Golder and his family did not choose to leave Salina until November, 1946. He accepted a position of rector of St. Elizabeth's Church in Glencoe, Illinois. In 1953, he again moved his ministry to Vallejo, California, where he was rector of the Church of Ascension. Two years later, he was called to St. Clement's Church in Seattle, where he stayed as rector until 1960.

Dean Golder retired from the Church of the Advent of Christ the King in San Francisco, California, in 1973, and died in El Granado, California, in March, 1985.

☩

FREDERIC WILLIAMS LITCHMAN
1947-1973

Born in Marblehead, Massachusetts, which he insisted had been named after him, Frederic W. Litchman came to

The Very Reverend Frederic W. Litchman. 1947-1973.

Christ Cathedral as its tenth Dean. He remained at Christ Cathedral for twenty-six years, far and away, the longest tenure of any Dean in the Cathedral's history.

After receiving a degree from Colorado State Teachers' College in Greeley, Litchman entered General Theological Seminary in New York. He graduated from there and was ordained to the priesthood in February, 1934.

He answered his first call from Grace Church, Ottawa, Kansas, where he was a rector for four years. He served a number of small parishes in southeastern Kansas, before being called to Grace Church in Chanute. The Litchman family left there when he was called to become Dean of the Cathedral in 1947.

When he arrived in Salina, the Cathedral had 145 communicants, and when he retired in 1973, that number had risen to over 400. During his twenty-six years as Dean, he was involved in the lives of hundreds of parishioners, having officiated at 745 baptisms, prepared 839 persons for Holy Confirmation, presided at 217 weddings, and read the burial service for more than 400 departed souls. He continued to compile statistics after his retirement, serving the Cathedral as its first Dean Emeritus, and acting as supply priest for parishes in Beloit, Hays, Great Bend, and other missions throughout the Diocese.

Dean Litchman first knew the present Diocese as the Missionary District of Salina, then later as the Missionary District of Western Kansas, and worked under the authority of three Bishops: The Right Reverends Shirley Nichols (1941-1956), Arnold M. Lewis (1956-1965), and William Davidson (1966-1980). During Dean Litchman's so-called retirement, he was under the jurisdiction of The Right Reverend John F. Ashby.

It was during his tenure that the awkward governing structure of the Cathedral Chapter was dissolved in 1961. The church, while remaining the seat of the Bishop, reverted to its original parish status under control of a dean-rector and vestry.

In 1963, Dean Litchman and the vestry hired an assistant for the Cathedral, The Reverend William Smythe. Fr. Smythe was hired at $4800, plus auto and utility expenses. However, by July 1964, the need for a fulltime assistant had waned, and funds were less than what was needed to support him. Clergy from St. Francis Boys' Home were able to help out when a need for extra clergy arose.

Several organizations were begun

Dean Litchman blesses children at the High Altar rail, following Daily Vacation Bible School. This photograph appeared on the cover of The Living Church, *national publication of the Episcopal Church, July, 1953.*

under the leadership of the Dean. The Junior Daughters of the King was organized as a complement to the Altar Guild, and high school-age girls of the church were introduced to the care and upkeep of the work in the sacristy. St. Vincent's Guild was formed for acolytes, layreaders and ushers, all of whom contributed much to church services. In 1968, the parish elected Mrs. Richard (Georgeanne) Dreher as first vestrywoman in the history of the Cathedral.

Dean Litchman instituted the observance of the Maundy Thursday Vigil, the *Tre Ores* (Three Hours) service on Good Friday, three liturgies on Sunday mornings, and regular weekday worship. A departure from his predecessor, Dean Litchman preferred a less formal, yet dignified, liturgy. The Dean's sermons were handwritten by him on scratch paper, and during one sermon he realized that part of his sermon was missing. He abruptly ended by saying, "My 'pearls of wisdom' are simply not here, and that's all you get today." He later discovered a member of the altar guild had written a note on what she assumed was scratch paper.

The Cathedral interior and grounds were considerably changed and updated during the tenure of Dean Litchman. Under his guidance and direction, a series of memorials provided the funds for the installation of stained glass windows in the nave and chapel. Through other thank-offerings, fund-raising projects and memorial donations, the bells in the tower were electrified, carpeting was installed, chandeliers replaced naked light bulbs, the organ was rebuilt, the sacristy redesigned, and the Cathedral was airconditioned. In addition, the women of the church produced needlepoint work to add beauty to the chancel, Bishop's throne and the chapel. Men of the church, particularly Hal Kinsley, who were skilled in woodworking, did considerable refurbishing of church furniture and crafted such items as hymn boards, the Christmas creche, and the large cross which hangs over the fireplace in the parish house.

The parish house, begun in the term of Dean Golder, was completed in 1948, a memorial from Irene Putnam. The Sunday School building was constructed in 1956, providing much needed office space, an area for storage, a nursery, and a number of Sunday School classrooms.

Dean Litchman first lived at the deanery at 150 South Eighth Street, with his wife, Martha, and their four children, Frances Ellen, William, Martha Linda, and John. They later moved to 824 Highland, where Martha Litchman died in December, 1975. In her memory, the Dean renovated the Cathedral Library in the parish house, and provided an endowment for its maintenance and the purchase of books. In November 1976, he and Helen C. Lindsey, longtime member of the congregation, were married.

The Dean was a supporter of the Salina Community Theater, and at one time took a role as a juror in the Theater's production *Twelve Angry Men*, by Reginald Rose. It was said that if he had stepped to the footlights and said, "The Lord be with you", that much of the audience would have responded, "And with thy spirit" and dropped to their knees.

Well into his retirement, the Dean continued to serve Christ Cathedral as Dean Emeritus, being particularly responsible for the 9:00 Eucharist on Thursday mornings. He regularly assisted at other services as well.

Perhaps the ministry of Frederic W. Litchman is best summarized by the text of a resolution passed by the vestry in September, 1973, following the announcement of Dean Litchman's retirement. It reads:

"Rector of this cathedral parish for more than a generation, pastor of its people in sickness and in health, comforting them in times of tribulation, rejoicing with them in times of joy, befriending the friendless, teaching, exhorting, loving, The Very Reverend Frederic W. Litchman had been a priest of the Church of God, earnestly following the examples of the Apostles.

He has served well the parish, the cathedral, the community, the diocese, and the Church, all to the Greater Glory of God.

Therefore, be it resolved by the Vestry of Christ Cathedral Parish, in recognition of the great service of The Very Reverend Frederic W. Litchman, that it pay formal tribute to him, that he be given a copy of this resolution duly subscribed, and that it be spread upon the permanent minutes of this parish."

An additional tribute was paid the Dean Emeritus in 1983 when a stone wall was erected as a Ninth Street entrance to the Cathedral Close. The wall connected the Cathedral and the parish house buildings, with an arched gateway in the center. It was designated the Litchman Gate, and dedicated to the ministry of Frederic W. Litchman.

Dean Litchman's death on January 7, 1992, at the age of eighty-six, followed a long illness. He was remembered by Father M. Richard Hatfield, the

The Very Reverend Sylvan W. Law. 1973-1979.

thirteenth Dean, at his funeral Mass, attended by over 300 people from around the country and including many from other faiths. His ashes were placed in the Columbarium in the Blessed Sacrament Chapel, now called the Chapel of St. Michael.

Dean Litchman also established two scholarship funds to help applicants to St. John's Military School and St. Francis Academy. He set up endowments for each of these purposes.

✠

SYLVAN WATSON LAW
1973-1979

Succeeding a man who had been Dean of Christ Cathedral for twenty-six years was a formidable task, but the

Dean Litchman stands by the wall erected in honor of his ministry, 1983.

Reverend Sylvan W. Law accepted the call and became the eleventh Dean of Christ Cathedral on December 1, 1973. He chose the first Sunday after Christmas of that year as the date for his installation.

A native of Miami, Florida, Dean Law graduated from the University of Miami and Virginia Polytechnic Institute in 1951. After a three year tour of duty with the United States Navy, he taught briefly at high school and college levels before entering Virginia Theological Seminary. He graduated from there in 1956. After his ordination as priest later that year, he began his ministry at parishes in Arkansas, and then began a nine-year service in the Diocese of Missouri. Dean Law then moved to Junction City, Kansas as rector of the Church of the Covenant before coming to Salina.

The new Dean had been active in both civic and diocesan affairs. In 1972, he was coordinator of the Anglican-Roman Catholic Clergy Day, which involved priests of both churches throughout Kansas. With his wife Evelyn, and their three children, the new Cathedral Dean made his home at 919 Sunrise Drive in Salina.

Dean Law soon realized that he had come to the Cathedral at a crucial point in its history. The time had arrived when extensive repairs had to be made to the building itself, and the vestry had unanimously decided to proceed with the capital repairs, as well as raising funds for a new organ. Dean Law kicked off the Cathedral Restoration Campaign in 1976, announcing that more than $102,000 had already been collected. The report on the condition of the building, made by Wilson and Company Engineers, revealed that work needed included spot sandblasting, pointing, waterproofing the exterior, repairs to the roof, new doors, plaster and painting.

It was during the Dean's tenure that the people of Christ Cathedral joined the rest of the nation in celebration of the American Bicentennial. On Sunday, July 4, 1976, the Eucharist was taken from the 1622 English Book of Common Prayer — the edition in use at the time of the American Revolution. A historical exhibit in the parish house included photographs, newspaper clippings, early communion silver and other items related to the beginning of the Episcopal Church in Salina. That afternoon, the Cathedral chimes were played for two minutes, along with the bells of other churches in Salina and across the land.

Dean and Mrs. Law researched and organized an Anglican Heritage Tour to England and Scotland in 1978. The focus was on the more than 1500 years of church history, and gave the participants an Anglican overview in their pilgrimage.

The Parish Council was established by Dean Law, with representatives of every organization in the parish. He emphasized planning by the laity, and the Council was designed to foster mutual support for the church's activities. Dean Law also originated a Visitation Training Workshop, where parishioners from the Church of the Incarnation, Salina; St Anne's, McPherson; Grace Church, Hutchinson; and Cathedral members could receive training for accommodating special needs within their congregations.

Because of his own historical and ecumenical interest, the Dean used every opportunity to widen the vision of the Cathedral congregation. One such opportunity occurred in June 1977, when the Cathedral was the site of a

Greek Orthodox wedding. The daughter of Mr. and Mrs. Stavropoulos of Salina was married by a Greek Orthodox priest from Overland Park. Following the ceremony, a celebration on the Cathedral grounds featured music and dancing according to the Greek custom. The Cathedral congregation was invited as observers and participants.

On the Diocesan level, Dean Law served on the Diocesan Council, the Trustees of Church Property Committee, led alcoholic treatment seminars, and was editor of the Western Kansas newsletter from 1975 to 1979.

In the spring of 1979, Dean Law accepted a call as vicar for the Church of the Redeemer in Delano, California. The Law family left Salina in March, and they now reside in Oregon.

✠

ARTHUR JOHN RATHBUN, Jr.
1979-1987

When Dean Sylvan Law decided to relocate, the Cathedral looked no further than the city limits for his replacement. The Reverend Arthur J. Rathbun, priest-in-charge for the Church of the Incarnation, accepted the call to the Dean's stall, and became the twelfth dean, in August, 1979.

Dean Rathbun was no stranger to the Cathedral, due to his work in the Diocese with a project called Venture in Mission, an undertaking in fund-raising. His ministerial background included some work in team ministry at the college level, as well as serving as vicar in church in Pennsylvania. The Dean had graduated from Pennsylvania State University in 1959, and General Theological Seminary in 1962, and was ordained in June of that year. Before

The Very Reverend Arthur J. Rathbun. 1979-1987.

coming to Kansas, he had been chaplain at two colleges in Pennsylvania.

Dean Rathbun served as Cathedral Dean during the episcopacies of two Bishops – William Davidson and John Ashby. In 1981, Bishop Ashby terminated the use of the 1928 Book of Common Prayer, and Dean Rathbun presided at the Cathedral during this period of change. The Cathedral parish continued to grow, in spite of this problem, and numbered 450 communicants in 1984.

Adult education during Dean Rathbun's time was centered on the Cursillo Movement, which gained popularity around the Diocese. The Dean instituted the Saturday evening service, and provided non-parochial priests with regularly scheduled services. For the first time, girls began participating as acolytes, and the number of women layreaders increased. Under the Dean's guidance, Sally Lambert was ordained to the diaconate at the Cathedral in 1983.

Renovation begun on the Cathedral building continued, and a major addition was the columbarium, built into the east wall of the Blessed Sacrament Chapel (now called St. Michael's) as the result of a memorial bequest. A stone wall was built connecting the Cathedral and parish house, with an archway leading to Ninth Street. This structure was dedicated in honor of the Dean Emeritus, Frederic W. Litchman.

Recognizing that maintenance of the Cathedral building would be a never-ending need, Dean Rathbun asked that an endowment fund be established for such a purpose. He considered this the major accomplishment of his tenure as Dean, observing that such a fund would provide means for capital maintenance and preservation of the building, and a way to avoid crisis maintenance.

Dean Rathbun's interest turned to family counseling in his final years as Cathedral Dean. He began preparations for a career change in this direction through studies and degree work at Kansas State University, Manhattan. His last Sunday recorded in the service register was on May 24, 1987. Deacon Sally Lambert had also, by this time, moved on to the Diocese of Oregon.

☩

M. RICHARD HATFIELD
1988 -

Assuming position as number thirteen in the list of Deans of Christ Cathedral, The Reverend M. Richard Hatfield was the first native Kansan to occupy the Dean's stall. Born in

The Very Reverend Richard Hatfield. 1988- .

Arkansas City, and a graduate of Southwestern College in Winfield, Dean Hatfield graduated from Nashotah House with a Master's of Divinity degree in 1978. In April of that year, on the Feast of St. Mark, he was ordained deacon at St. David's Church, Topeka, by the Bishop of Kansas, with The Most Reverend and Right Honorable Michael Ramsey, the one-hundredth Archbishop of Canterbury, as the preacher.

Dean Hatfield was ordained to the priesthood on All Saints' Day, November 1, 1978, at St. Michael and All Angels' Church in Denver. He was the Curate of the parish and also chaplain to St. Anne's Episcopal School, Denver. In 1981, following his marriage to Shelley Gray, the Dean answered a call to serve the Anglican Province of Southern

African in the Diocese of Pretoria.

Duties in South Africa began as Divinity Master and Chaplain at St. Mary's Diocesan School for Girls. Fr. Hatfield, at the same time, also started a new church, called Corpus Christi, at Garsfontein. The new congregation grew from mission to parish status in only one year.

In the turbulent years of apartheid in South Africa, the Hatfields, with sons Jason and Sean, had difficulty with the government and the required permanent resident permit. In June on 1985, the Dean and his family returned to Nashotah House where he earned the Master of Sacred Theology degree in liturgics.

In 1986, Hatfield and his family moved to Logansport, Indiana, where he accepted a call as rector of Trinity Church. Two years later, he was approached by Bishop John F. Ashby, whom he encountered at the General Convention, held in Detroit that year, about the vacancy at Christ Cathedral. The Hatfields came to Salina in August of 1988 to have a look at the Cathedral, and recognizing the enormous potential, accepted the challenging position. The Hatfields arrived in Salina in December. The Cathedral had been nineteen months without a dean. The Reverend Robert Hutchinson served as interim for twelve months in 1987 and 1988.

Dean Hatfield set about restoring Anglo-Catholic liturgy to the Cathedral and re-established the public offering of the Daily Office. Adherence to the Church kalendar became the norm again, with special emphasis placed on Holy Days and the Marian feasts. The Society of Mary grew into the Chapter of the Nativity of the Blessed Virgin Mary, and the Order of St. Vincent, a guild for acolytes and other lay servers, was restored.

The Cathedral began to reach out to the Diocese in fulfillment of Bishop Griswold's vision of the Cathedral Church as the Mother Church of the Diocese. A good working relationship with St. Francis Academy and St. John's Military School was re-established in this time. In 1989, the Dean served St. John's as chaplain, drawing on his previous service as a school chaplain, and in 1991, he became a member of the board of S.J.M.S. While serving the Cathedral, the Dean also ventured out in the wilds of western Kansas to cover congregations without a priest. His travels took him to Scott City, Russell Springs, Ulysses, Hugoton, Hutchinson and Bennington. In 1992, the Church of the Transfiguration in Bennington officially came under the care of the Cathedral.

Through memorials and gifts, stained glass windows were provided for the choir room and acolyte room; vestments were restored and additions were made; and the Cathedral offices were refurbished. Associates of the Sisterhood of the Holy Nativity grew in number. Photographs of past bishops and deans and significant church documents were framed and placed in the north and south corridors of the cathedral.

Dean Hatfield became involved with the creation of Ashby House, a shelter for homeless families on the adjacent Church property, and serves as president of its executive board. He also fills various roles in the structure of the Diocese of Western Kansas, including being a General Convention Deputy and President of the Standing Committee.

Sharing pastoral responsibilities with the Dean is The Reverend Canon Joseph M. Kimmett, who came to the Cathedral as curate in 1990, after his graduation from Nashotah House in

May. Fr. Kimmett was ordained deacon at his home parish of St. Michael and All Angels' in Denver on May 31, 1990, by The Right Reverend William Wolfrum. He was ordained priest in Salina on December 7, 1990, by Bishop Ashby. His duties have been focused in the areas of Christian education; acolytes and liturgy; and youth work, a program in need of revival before his arrival. At his instigation, members of the Cathedral formed a softball team, named The Holy Smokes, and entered competition in a local league. Born in Denver, and a 1984 graduate of the School of Journalism at the University of Colorado in Boulder, Fr. Kimmett also assumed responsibility for church mailings, such as *The Cathedral Times,* a new weekly newsletter from the Cathedral office. During the summer of 1991, Fr. Kimmett spent five weeks in Kent County, England, serving as priest-in-charge for a parish ten minutes from Canterbury.

With these accomplishments, the tenure of Dean Hatfield has already revitalized the Cathedral. About his future expectations, the Dean says, "Dean Litchman, just prior to his death, told me that the Cathedral was once again being truly faithful to her original vocation as a center of liturgical life and pastoral care. I pray that this is true, and in addition to being faithful to the original vision of Bishop Griswold and Mrs. Batterson, we can become not only a place of external beauty, but a place known to be filled with faithful Christians who love Jesus and His Church and proclaim the full-blooded Catholic faith without apology."

The moment of the laying on of the hands at the ordination of Fr. Kimmett, December 7, 1990

VI. Bishops

The saying is sure: If any one aspires to the office of bishop, he desires a noble task. Now a bishop must be above reproach, the husband of one wife, temperate, sensible, dignified, hospitable, an apt teacher, no drunkard, not violent but gentle, not quarrelsome, and no lover of money. He must manage his own household well, keeping his children submissive and respectful in every way; for if a man does not know how to manage his own household, how can he care for God's church? — 1 Timothy 3:1-5

SHELDON MUNSON GRISWOLD
1903-1917

The first bishop named to the Missionary District of Salina was The Right Reverend Sheldon Munson Griswold. His main concern upon his arrival was the erection of a cathedral building. In this pursuit he had the spiritual and financial support of many friends from his former parishes in New York, and particularly from Mrs. Sarah E. Batterson.

Bishop Griswold had a firmly established background in New York. He was born in Delhi, New York on July 8, 1861, and graduated from General Theological Seminary in 1885. That same year he married Kate M. van der Bogart, and began his ministry, serving parishes in Ilion, Mohawk, and Frankfort, New York. In 1890 he accepted a call to Hudson, New York, where he first met Mrs. Sarah Batterson, a devout laywoman from Philadelphia. He served the church in Hudson, first as rector, then as archdeacon. In 1903, at the age of forty two, Bishop Griswold was consecrated bishop in Albany, New York.

He quoted one of the bishops that consecrated him in his address to the clergy and laity at the first annual convocation in Salina, when he said, "He that ploweth must plow in hope." He added, "Let us hope in Him who has called us to this work, in whom we believe. It is a great work which has been entrusted to us, and, while we are not responsible for results of our work, we are exactly responsible for our faithfulness and our zeal, which must be tempered by wisdom."

As a missionary bishop, Bishop Griswold envisioned a strong ministry, while recognizing his was a difficult situation. At every attempt, he was setting new precedence. His was an untried

The Right Reverend Sheldon Munson Griswold. 1903-1917.

position, and the success or failure of the Missionary District of Salina related directly to his efforts. He made many trips east in search of funding. His strongest ally in his endeavor to build a cathedral in the missionary field was found in Mrs. Batterson. The young Bishop's dream of a cathedral in the English style was realized mainly through her generosity and support of his churchmanship and ministry.

At the first service in the new cathedral building, Bishop Griswold had this to say, "We must bear in our minds this fact, that this building, reared first of all for the worship of God, is not merely for the use of the people in the District of Salina who belong to our own communion, but for the use of the whole community — and for the absolute use of all those who seek to find rest for their souls, and to lift their hearts in prayer to Almighty God to pardon their sins. It is more than that, too; it is the center of unity for the whole of the Church within the Missionary District of Salina — which we hope will sometime grow to be the Diocese."

Bishop Griswold, of course, did not limit his concerns to construction of a cathedral. He traveled hundreds of miles throughout the then Missionary District of Salina to open new work, or to offer encouragement and support to the lonely missionaries stationed at the outposts. The foresight of the Bishop did not go unnoticed, and he assumed leadership in community affairs as well. In 1909 he undertook the building of a hospital to serve Salina, and later spearheaded a drive to construct the first YMCA in Salina.

In January, 1917 Bishop Griswold was elected Suffragan Bishop of the Diocese of Chicago, and left his work in Salina to begin duties there. He served that Diocese until 1930, when he was named Bishop. However, his tenure as Bishop lasted only ten months, when he died in November of that year. Bishop Griswold was buried at Memorial Park Cemetery in Chicago on December 2, 1930 at age sixty nine years old.

The Church in Salina and throughout Western Kansas, as well as the City of Salina, are forever in the debt of this energetic young bishop. During his time in Salina, he forever changed the look of the city when the Cathedral tower was added to the skyline. His guidance and direction gave the Missionary District a firm footing so that it eventually could become the Diocese he envisioned in his speech at the Cathedral's first service.

The love Bishop Sheldon M. Griswold had for the Cathedral was evidenced in his will, when his personal crucifix was added to the beauty of the Cathedral. Indeed, Bishop Griswold did "plow in hope", and this hope still thrives today.

✠

JOHN CHARLES SAGE
1918 - 1919

To follow in the steps of a strong leader and energetic man such as Bishop Griswold would be the envy of few. The second bishop of the Missionary District of Salina was the Right Reverend John Charles Sage. In one short year he demonstrated the zeal and dedication to follow Griswold. Tragically, though, his episcopate was shortened by his early death.

A native of Ohio, John Charles Sage was consecrated as Bishop of the District of Salina in January of 1918 at his former parish in Iowa. He was installed at Christ Cathedral with a cadet corps from St. John's Military School present for the ceremonies. The former Bishop, Sheldon Griswold, officiated.

Bishop Sage was born in Cleveland in 1866, and entered Western Theological Seminary in Chicago. He was ordained deacon in 1891, and was ordained to the priesthood in 1893. He served mission churches in Illinois, and became rector of St. John's Church in Keokuk, Iowa in 1902. It was from there he received the call to serve Salina as Bishop.

After moving to Salina with his wife, the former Harriet Louise Murphey, and his daughter, Bishop Sage considered the Bishop's residence on South Santa Fe to be too large and expensive. That property, in the 500 block of South Santa Fe, was sold to Dan Wiegner, and the property at Eighth and Walnut Streets was purchased from Mrs.

The Right Reverend John Charles Sage. 1918-1919.

Florence Shellabarger, along with the north seventy five feet of lots numbered 135-138, for $12,000. The Domestic and Foreign Missionary Society lent the District of Salina $10,000 of that amount at five percent interest.

Bishop Sage had to deal with the loss of the dean of his cathedral in February, 1918, when a letter of resignation was received from Dean George B. Kinkead. In spite of a petition signed by 103 parishioners asking that the resignation not be accepted, the Bishop determined it was in the best interests of the church to accept the resignation.

Services at the cathedral became sporadic, with Bishop Sage officiating as often as possible. By July, only Sunday and Thursday Eucharists were held. The influenza epidemic cancelled services in October and December of that year. On Christmas Eve, 1918, the 11:30 pm service would be the last Midnight Mass until 1925.

The Bishop reported the "with no one else in view", he would fill the cathedral's pulpit, and, on Easter Day, 1919, the Mass was celebrated twice in the morning, and a children's service was held in the afternoon.

Following a summer vacation, Bishop Sage was stricken ill and hospitalized in Chicago. Even though he was confined to bed, upon his return to Salina he continued to conduct the business of the Cathedral and the District of Salina. He died at his home on October 2, 1919. The Bishop's funeral service was conducted at the Cathedral the following Sunday.

The acting Bishop for the Missionary District was the Rt. Rev. George Beecher, Bishop of Nebraska, who visited Salina in mid-October, and nominated the Rev. W.D. Morrow, then Canon-in-Residence, as the Priest-in-Charge of the Cathedral.

Without a dean, the people decided to hold services in the Guild House, partly because there was no coal to heat the Cathedral, and because there was no money with which to buy any. The situation was dire, and, records show that on Christmas Day, 1919, attendance was only sixty six persons.

An Every-Member Canvass generated enough funds in February, 1920, so that the Chapter asked Bishop Beecher to make nominations for a Dean, "in view of the amount of the pledges made by members and friends of the Cathedral parish." Bishop Beecher responded with a $300 check to be applied to the coal bill, and to what the Cathedral owed to its former Dean, George Kinkead.

ROBERT HERBERT MIZE
1921-1938

The young Missionary District of Salina had been without a bishop of its own for fifteen months before the Right Reverend Robert Herbert Mize was consecrated. In an era of World War and national depression, Bishop Mize would prove to be a Godsend to the faithful of western Kansas.

St. John's Military School was responsible for first bringing Mize to Salina as Headmaster of the school, in 1898. Born in Chicago in 1870, Bishop Mize moved to Atchison, Kansas, at an early age. His family helped establish the wholesale hardware firm of Blish, Mize, and Silliman. The young Mize acquired his business acumen there.

The Mize family were members of Trinity Church, Atchison, and Robert Mize entered General Theological Seminary following graduation from St. Stephen's College. He was ordained in 1897, and served St. John's Church in Hiawatha, Kansas as rector for one year before accepting the position at St. John's Military School.

Fr. Mize returned to New York in 1903 and married Margaret T. Moore. She could boast that every male relative she had was an Episcopal clergyman, not knowing that her own two sons would be ordained by their father after her death.

After eight years at St. John's as Headmaster, Mize accepted a call to St. Andrew's Church in Emporia, Kansas, where he would serve for six years. In 1912, the Mize family moved again to answer a call at St. Paul's in Kansas City. It was from this church that Fr. Mize accepted the call to become Bishop of the Missionary District of Western Kansas in 1921.

The Right Reverend Robert Herbert Mize. 1921-1938.

The decision was not an easy one. The District was in financial straits following the death of Bishop Sage in 1919, and Bishop Mize was warned by his brother-in-law, dean of Trinity Cathedral, Cleveland, that the Missionary District was "the most difficult and discouraging field in the Episcopal Church." Furthermore, Mrs. Mize was ill with tuberculosis. In spite of these considerations, Robert H. Mize consented to be Bishop of the Missionary District of Salina. His consecration was held in Topeka on January 19, 1921; Bishop Sheldon M. Griswold was one of his consecrators.

The Mize family moved into the Bishop's quarters at 8th and Walnut

Streets, and their two sons, Edward and Robert, were enrolled at St. John's Military School. Mrs. Mize's health continued to decline, and she moved to Denver, where she died in 1923. A housekeeper cared for the Mize's daughter, "little Margaret."

Addressing the Convention of the Missionary District in 1922, Bishop Mize pointed out the serious financial conditions and established an endowment fund for the Episcopate. He also provided generous personal financial support for the Cathedral.

Bishop Mize served the Missionary District for seventeen years, resigning in 1938. He moved to Arizona in his retirement, living with his daughter's family and remaining closely in touch with his two sons — The Reverend Edward Mize, Chief of Chaplains in Washington, D.C., and The Reverend Robert Mize, Jr., founder of St. Francis Boys' Homes in Salina.

After his death in April, 1956, the body of Bishop Mize was returned to Salina for his funeral service and interment at Gypsum Hill Cemetery in Salina, where his wife and infant twin sons are buried also. The stained glass window in the north transept of the Cathedral was given by the Mize children, in memory of their parents.

It must be said that Bishop Mize accepted a call from a struggling missionary district, and left it in much sounder condition than he found it. The Cathedral, too, greatly profited from the work of this third Bishop.

To fill the gap between bishops, The Right Reverend Nelson Spencer, Bishop of West Missouri, served the Missionary District of Western Kansas for two years until a new bishop was secured.

✠

SHIRLEY HALL NICHOLS
1941-1956

The retirement of Bishop Mize in 1938 again left the Missionary District without local pastoral leadership. The arrival of the fourth bishop, however, was due more to events on the international scene than anything on the prairie lands of the Smoky Hill River.

The Right Reverend Shirley Hall Nichols came to Salina as a result of the advent of World War II. He was born in New York in 1884, graduated from Harvard and then General Theological Seminary in 1911. Expressing his interest in working abroad, he was sent to Japan in 1914, under the direction of the Foreign Missionary Society of the

The Right Reverend Shirley Hall Nichols. 1941-1956

Episcopal Church.

While in Japan, Fr. Nichols served posts in Hirosake, Aomori, and Odate for twelve years. During this time he married Hasu H. Gardiner, and they reared a family of four children. In 1926, Nichols became Bishop of the Missionary

Bishop Nichols gives the blessing from the stage of the newly-constructed Parish House.

District of Kyoto. He held this position until 1940, when deteriorating political conditions forced the Nichols family to return to the United States. He was immediately appointed Acting-Bishop in 1941 for the vacant Missionary District of Salina, and two years later, the appointment became permanent. Bishop Nichols' experiences with the Japanese people had been nothing but pleasant, and he said in a newspaper interview, "I feel more at home preaching in Japanese than in English."

Because of his long tenure in Japan, he was especially concerned and distressed over the confinement of Japanese-Americans on the west coast, and so expended considerable effort in various attempts to alleviate their plight. He also showed considerable interest in the problems of American servicemen stationed near Salina, as well as various alien prisoners of war located at camps within the Missionary District. Following the close of the war, he was active in the readjustment problems of military and civilian personnel.

Among the casualties of World War II was the Nichols' daughter, Cecil, who was killed in a plane crash in Perth, Australia, while working for the American Red Cross. A stained glass window in the Cathedral was given by her parents in 1946.

Following his retirement in 1956, Bishop and Mrs. Nichols moved to New Jersey, near his boyhood home. He maintained an active interest in church affairs until his death in February, 1964.

In April of that year, the Executive Board of the Missionary District of Western Kansas established a Memorial Fund in the memory of Bishop Nichols, which was contributed to the building of the Episcopal Church Center in New York City. The memorial plaque in that building reads as follows:

SHIRLEY HALL NICHOLS
1884-1964

Bishop of Kyoto
1926-1940

Bishop of Salina
1941-1956

Memorialized by
Western Kansas

✠

ARNOLD M. LEWIS
1956-1965

The first bishop to be consecrated in Christ Cathedral, The Right Reverend Arnold M. Lewis was elected to fill the vacancy in the Missionary District left by the retirement of Bishop Nichols. A New York native, Bishop Lewis received his Theological degree from Virginia Theological Seminary, and completed graduate work from both Union and General seminaries in New York. He was ordained both deacon and priest in 1936.

First serving St. Mark's Church, Long Island, Bishop Lewis enlisted in the U.S. Army as a chaplain in 1940. After service at military installations throughout the world, he remained in the Active Reserve with the rank of Lieutenant Colonel. Following his military service, he became Executive Director of the Presiding Bishop's Committee on Laymen's Work, which he did for five years. In 1951 he became dean of St. John's Cathedral in Jacksonville, Florida, and it was from there he was elected Bishop for Salina.

For his consecration at Christ Cathedral, February 1956, fourteen bishops and more than thirty priests took part in the ceremonies. The Most Reverend Henry Knox Sherrill, Presiding Bishop, was the chief consecrator.

Bishop and Mrs. Lewis (Frances) and their two children made their home at 36 Crestview because of the deteriorating condition of the Bishop's House at Eighth and Walnut.

In a note of greeting, the retired Bishop Mize wrote from Arizona, "By the graciousness of a kindly Providence, I have been associated with the District as priest and bishop since it was set

The Right Reverend Arnold M. Lewis. 1956-1965.

Bishops process into Christ Cathedral for the consecration of Arnold Lewis, 1956.

apart from the Diocese of Kansas, and though now absent, I feel that I am one with the clergy and laity of the District in expressing to you a word of welcome to our beloved Church there, and our good wishes for the future....As I have now reached the age which prevents travel, I may not have the privilege of meeting you personally—but my interest will follow you and so will my prayers for you as you go forth to new work for Our Lord and His Church."

Bishop Lewis did not share the same Anglo-Catholic leanings of his predecessors. Indeed, it was rumored that the National Church saw his election as an opportunity to "shut down' the Missionary District. Nothing can be supported, but, in any case, the temperament of the District did shift during Lewis' episcopate. In 1960, the Missionary District changed its name from "Salina" to "Western Kansas".

Bishop Lewis saw as a main concern the need for a conference center in the District, a place where young people and adults could be trained for leadership roles. He wanted the location to be as centrally located as possible, so it was that Camp PECUSA (Protestant Episcopal Church of the United States of America) came into existence on the shore of Lake Webster, near Stockton, Kansas. It was later renamed the Arnold M. Lewis Conference Center.

Two policies were established at the formation of PECUSA. First, St. Mary's Chapel would be the center of camp life, and secondly, young people at camp would spend one hour each morning doing physical work on the premises, thereby enabling them to give something of themselves to the conference center.

Bishop Lewis also instituted training of lay readers within the District, to be known as the Bishop's Men. After completing a course of study, the men were installed at St. Mary's Chapel at PECUSA, each given a cross on a ribbon engraved with the words, "Bishop's Man - District of Western Kansas." In 1964, Bishop Lewis listed the roster of seventy-three Bishop's Men as "high on the list of accomplishments" for the District.

Later that year, a military service at St. John's Military School honored Bishop Lewis' retirement from the Army Reserve Chaplain Corps. The Bishop was promoted to full colonel, and after his silver wings were presented to him, a full-dress parade was held in his honor.

It was also in 1964, at Lewis' instigation, that the newly established Episcopal Church of the Incarnation opened its doors in south Salina, affording Salinans with a choice of Episcopal churches.

In 1965, Bishop Lewis accepted the position of Suffragan Bishop for the Armed forces, which he held until his retirement in 1970. He and Mrs. Lewis then made their home in Virginia and continued an interest in the affairs of Western Kansas, including a return visit to PECUSA in 1978.

During the time after Bishop Lewis left Salina, and before the consecration of Bishop William Davidson, the Missionary District of Western Kansas was served by The Right Reverend Edward Clark Turner, Bishop of the Diocese of Kansas. Bishop Turner supervised the business of the District, including confirmations.

WILLIAM DAVIDSON
1966-1980

With the Missionary District intact following the departure of Bishop Lewis, little time was lost before the Right Reverend William Davidson was called as the next bishop. Little did this son of a Montana rancher know that he would arrive as sixth bishop of the District and leave as first bishop of the Diocese of Western Kansas.

A graduate of Montana State University with a degree in agricultural education, Bishop Davidson first taught school in his home state. After marrying Mary Shoemaker, he entered the Berkley Divinity School and became a priest on April 25, 1947.

Davidson began his ministry as vicar-in-charge of a four-mission field in Montana. In 1951 he was called to become rector of St. James Church in Lewiston, Montana, and left there in 1956 to work for the national church offices in New York City. For the next six years he was Associate Secretary of the Division of Town and Country within the Home Department of the Executive Council of the Episcopal Church.

In 1962 he resigned to return to rural ministry, becoming the rector of Grace Church, Jamestown, North Dakota. He was elected Bishop of the Missionary District of Salina by the House of Bishops in September, 1965.

At the invitation of the Sisters of St. Joseph and the Roman Catholic diocese of Salina, Bishop Davidson was consecrated on January 6, 1966, at the auditorium of Marymount College. He chose the site because it was a large facility. The Most Reverend John E. Hines, Presiding Bishop, was the consecrator,

The Right Reverend William Davidson. 1966-1980.

and former bishop, Arnold M. Lewis, participated and read the Gospel.

That afternoon, the new bishop was enthroned at Christ Cathedral, and a reception followed, sponsored by St. John's Military School and St. Francis Boys' Homes, two institutions with which the new bishop would become closely involved.

The new bishop, his wife Mary, and their four children, bought a house at 1004 Manor Road.

In keeping with his spirit of ecumenism, Bishop Davidson participated in many interdenominational groups. He was the first speaker at an ecumenical series at Kansas Wesleyan University; he was a delegate to the Great Plains Interreligious Council, and also served as member of the Great Plains Agricultural

Council. In 1968 he addressed the National Catholic Rural Life Conference and was active in the Rural Workers' Fellowship. He was president of the Kansas Council of Churches, and was locally active in the Salina Ministerium. On the national level, Bishop Davidson headed the Episcopal Committee on Conscientious Objectors to Military Service, serving in that capacity during the volatile Vietnam era.

During the late sixties and seventies the Book of Common Prayer was undergoing revision, and Bishop Davidson led the diocese through a series of trial rites. Although he favored the revisions, he impartially evaluated the reception of the proposed changes. He also favored the ordination of women to the priesthood, but was kept in check by the Commission on Ministry and Standing Committee of the Diocese.

At the General Convention of 1970, the Missionary District of Western Kansas submitted a petition for diocesan status. The petition was favorably received, and while Bishop Davidson was entitled to remain as the appointed bishop, he maintained that the new Diocese should have an elected bishop. So it was, at the first Diocesan Convention, held in Salina in 1971, delegates showed their love for William Davidson and elected him first Bishop of the Diocese of Western Kansas.

During his tenure, Bishop Davidson accepted responsibility at the Cathedral by assuming regularly scheduled services whenever possible, as well as other pastoral duties. He twice served the Cathedral as interim Dean — in the fall of 1973 after the retirement of Dean F.W. Litchman, and in 1979, following the resignation of Dean Sylvan Law.

In May, 1980, Bishop Davidson announced that he would accept a position as Assistant Bishop in the Diocese of Ohio. Citing a new enthusiasm and greater self-image for the Diocese of Western Kansas, Bishop Davidson determined that the time had come for new leadership for the Diocese.

Bishop Davidson and Mary later moved to Loveland, Colorado, where they would celebrate fifty years of marriage. He is now assisting the Bishop of Colorado.

✠

JOHN FORSYTHE ASHBY
1981-

Bishops had come to Western Kansas from all points of the compass, save the south. All that changed with the election of The Right Reverend John F. Ashby as second Bishop of the Diocese of Western Kansas. He came in 1981 to fill the vacancy left by Bishop William Davidson.

An Oklahoma native, John Ashby entered the Episcopal Theological Seminary of the Southwest, in Austin, Texas, following his graduation from Oklahoma State University in 1952. While attending seminary, he married Mary Carver. He was ordained a priest in 1955. He served parishes in rural Oklahoma and in 1959 answered a call from St. Luke's Church, Ada, Oklahoma, where he served as rector for more than twenty-two years.

The Reverend John Ashby was commissioned in the United Sates Army Chaplains' Corps in 1960, and for twenty-one years served as Chaplain in the Oklahoma National Guard. He retired from that duty in 1981, with the rank of Lieutenant Colonel. He served the Diocese of Oklahoma in many capacities, and in 1966-67 received a James

The Right Reverend John F. Ashby. 1981-

Mills Fellowship to study New Testament Ethics at the University of Cambridge, England.

Consecration ceremonies for the newly-elected Bishop were held in May, 1981, at St. John's Military School. The Most Reverend John M. Allin, Presiding Bishop, was chief consecrator, with former Western Kansas Bishop Davidson, and the Right Reverend William Wantland as co-consecrators. Bishop Ashby and Mary bought a house at 512 Sunset Drive in Salina, which became a gathering place for their two daughters, Ann and Elizabeth, and their families. In June, 1981, the Bishop was enthroned at Christ Cathedral during Evensong. Although he was counted as the second Bishop of the Diocese, Bishop Ashby became the seventh occupant of the Bishop's chair.

Maintaining his office at 142 South Eighth Street, just south of the Cathedral grounds, Bishop Ashby soon determined that the vast distances of the Diocese necessitated faster means of travel. With that, he received his pilot's license and took to the air to visit the more remote areas of the Diocese of Western Kansas.

The Bishop began a practice of ecumenical outreach on Easter Day, 1982, when he led the Cathedral choir and communicants to the Roman Catholic Sacred Heart Cathedral just half a block away, to exchange Easter greetings with Bishop Daniel W. Kucera and his congregation. The next year, directions were reversed, and Bishop Kucera, accompanied by members of the Knights of Columbus and clergy from Sacred Heart Cathedral, processed to Christ Cathedral. From the altar, both Bishops read Easter prayers and exchanged the Peace.

In 1984, Bishop Ashby moved the Diocesan offices out of the cramped headquarters near the Cathedral to a modern office complex in Executive Plaza, 1505 East Iron Street. That same year he returned to England to attend a lecture series at the University of Cambridge. In 1988 he joined his fellow Bishops from around the world at the Lambeth Conference, hosted by the Archbishop of Canterbury. In 1991, he was one of two American Bishops who attended a conference at the University of York on "Affirming Catholicism."

Bishop Ashby was elected to chair Coalition 14, a group of small dioceses, all former missionary districts. He also chairs the National Church Council for Development of Ministry.

In 1986 the Bishop asked for a three-month leave of absence during which time he and Mary moved to Guam where he was the interim-Bishop of Micronesia. While in Guam, he oversaw construction of a new church, and established a preaching station in Saipan. In 1989, he again served as an interim-Bishop, this time for the Diocese of Kansas, after the Right Reverend Richard Grein was elected Bishop of New York.

The Bishop belongs to several organizations, including the Irenaeus Fellowship, a group of bishops that meet to study and discuss the issues of the Church. He is also a member of the Bishops of Small Dioceses, and helps to facilitate their conferences in Dallas.

Bishop Ashby's name is among those on a list of retired military chaplains, kept by the Presiding Bishop. At the time of Desert Storm, during the 1991 war in Iraq, the retired chaplains were on standby, awaiting orders to go to Germany and relieve chaplains there for duty in the combat zone. He sits on the board of St. Francis Academy and is ex-officio on the board of St. John's Military School, both institutions headquartered in Salina. He also serves on the executive board of the Leadership Academy for New Directions, which provides training for rural clergy.

In Salina, Bishop Ashby's name appears on a shelter for homeless families. When organization began for such a shelter, which no other agency provided, the Bishop donated the former Deanery on South Eighth Street for the project. Bishop George Fitzsimons, Roman Catholic Bishop of Salina (who was involved in the project), suggested the name "Ashby House" as a show of gratitude.

A major accomplishment in the Bishop's outreach efforts has been the Migration Ministries,' helping to settle the thousands of refugees located in southwestern Kansas. A further accomplishment is that the Diocese operates with a balanced budget, partly because of the Bishop's efforts in applying for grants and fellowships to finance programs in clergy and laypersons training. The Diocese of Western Kansas has retained fairly constant population and congregation assessments.

The Bishop has ordained seventeen deacons, including four women, and eight priests since his own consecration in 1981. The work of Bishop Ashby in Western Kansas is not finished, and people of the Diocese can expect more from this man from Oklahoma.

Bishop Ashby prepares Yorkshire Pudding for a meal featuring British food.

ALL HAIL THE POWER OF JESUS' NAME 79

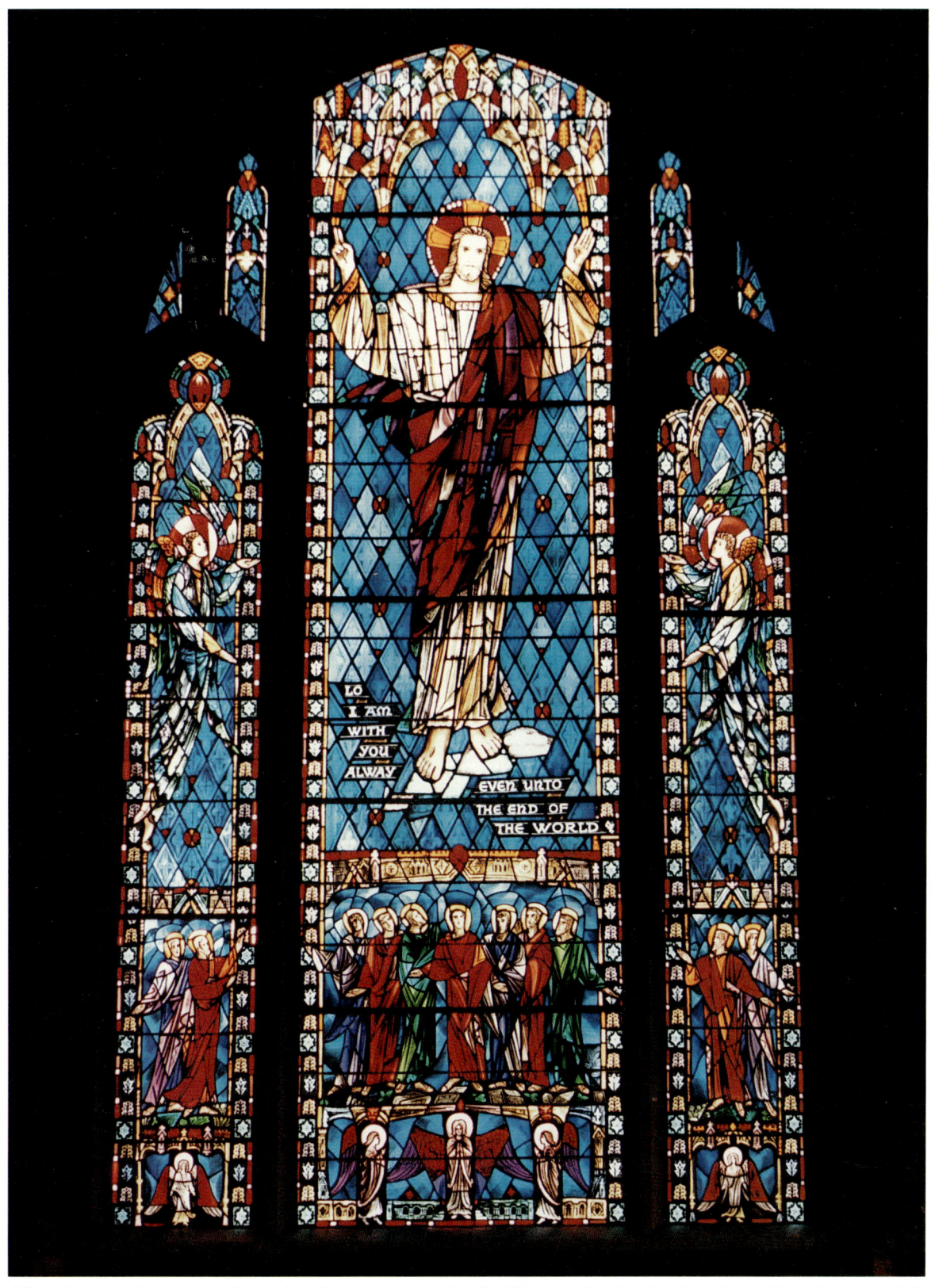

The Ascension window in the east end of Christ Cathedral, given by the parish family, 1961.

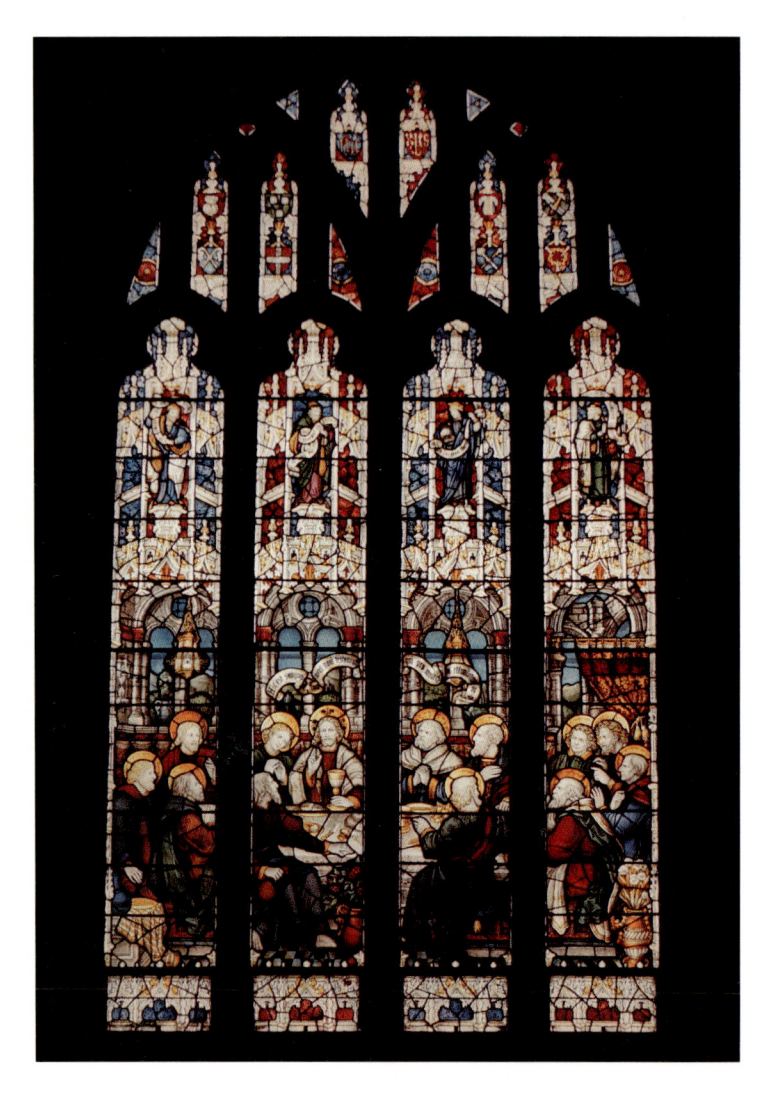

The Last Supper, stained glass from the Kempe Co., London, given by Dean Kinkead.

"The Worship of Heaven", Christ the King enthroned, with the Archangels Michael and Gabriel on the west wall, given by the parish family between 1912 and 1925

ALL HAIL THE POWER OF JESUS' NAME 81

Karlee Gray and other Sunday School students and teachers plant a garden in the Cathedral Park, 1991.

The Altar of Repose at the St. Mary Altar on Maundy Thursday, 1992.

82 ALL HAIL THE POWER OF JESUS' NAME

Christ Cathedral, decorated for Easter, 1991.

The Baptismal font in the South Transept, decorated for Easter.

Parishioners prepare for races at the Pentecost Fete, 1991.

The crafts booth at the annual Pentecost Fete.

Cathedral Acolytes and Lay Eucharistic Ministers, 1991.
Front: Jennifer Favre, Grant Hays, Parker Wallace, David Litchman, Sean Hatfield, Fr. Kimmett, Jason Peterson. Middle: Jerry Favre, Marcia Anderson, Jon Favre, Courtney Stockham, Elizabeth Miller, Ryan Wallace. Back: Vernon Osborn, Fr. Hatfield, Kass Gray, Brian Kruckemyer, Steve Hays, Barbara Young, Lee Wilbur, Jason Hatfield, Michael Woods, Jack Lambert, Kent Berquist.

Newly installed Cathedral Canons, 1992.
Left to right, Fr. Philip Rapp, Fr. Joseph Kimmett, Msgr. Raymond Menard, Fr. James Cox; background, Fr. Richard Hatfield, Bp. John Ashby, Bp. George Fitzsimons.

ALL HAIL THE POWER OF JESUS' NAME 85

Dedication of flag poles at the Cathedral in honor of Col. Keith Duckers, SJMS. (Duckers is to right of pole), 1991.

Ascension Day and Feast of Dedication 1992, left to right, Fr. Joseph Kimmett, Fr. Richard Hatfield, Bp. Patrick Matalengwe, Fr. James Cox.

86 ALL HAIL THE POWER OF JESUS' NAME

Crucifix at the 12th Station, Outdoor Columbarium and Stations of the Cross, Cathedral Park.

Christ Cathedral from the air.

VII. Friends Around Town

For as in one body we have many members, and all the members do not have the same function, so we, though many, are one body in Christ, and individually members one of another. Having gifts that differ according to the grace given to us, let us use them: if prophecy, in proportion to our faith; if service, in our serving; he who teaches, in his teaching; he who exhorts, in his exhortation; he who contributes, in liberality; he who gives aid, with zeal; he who does acts of mercy, with cheerfulness.
— Romans 12:4-8

No Christian organization can, or should, exist purely for itself, for to do so defeats the purpose of reaching out and proclaiming the Good News. Rendering service unto Almighty God is the primary objective of a church, but extending the love of God to fellow man is also of great importance. Christ Cathedral, from her very beginning, has always looked outward, providing support to worthy causes in Salina, around the country, and around the world. One often thinks of outreach as merely helping the poor and downcast, but it is in fact much more. Space wouldn't permit detailed accounts of the many ventures with which Christ Cathedral has been involved. For the sake of brevity, five different examples will be discussed, not only because they are well-known, but because they exemplify the nature of the relationship between a cathedral and those who look for support. Support, of course, isn't only defined as financial giving, but extends beyond monetary considerations to spiritual and moral support.

Saint John's Military School

Many years before Bishop Griswold arrived in Salina, or the idea of a cathedral had been conceived, the Episcopal Church had established St. John's Military School in north Salina. The credit for its founding belongs to The Right Reverend Elisha Smith Thomas, Coadjutor, and later second Bishop of Kansas (and for whom Thomas Park in Salina is named.) He had an idea for starting a militant Church school. Through his influence with a number of prominent businessmen, a charter was secured in 1887 by J.H. Prescott, Joseph A. Atrim, M.D. Teague, Arthur M. Claflin, A.F. Harsh, William Hogben and A.L. Dodge. Other incorporators included The Reverend E.P. Chittenden (Rector of Christ Church,) W.D. Christian, Hugh King and W.E. Ober, names which are familiar to Salinans and readers of Cathedral history.

A publication of St. John's, states the institution's goals:

An institution unique in Kansas history was founded a century ago when an Episcopal Bishop and a group of Salina businessmen saw the need for the disciplined environment of a military school under church auspices. With their books and Bibles, plus a strong determination that the education of young men should go forward along with the settlement of the frontier, these Christian leaders founded a school whose strength has

The Right Reverend Elisha Smith Thomas, Second Bishop of Kansas.

Early day cadets at St. John's Military School perform drill in parade area. Vail Hall stands in the background.

met the trials of all the yesterdays. Since the date of its founding, 1887, St. John's Military School has seen uniforms and times change. But the purpose — to help a boy work up to his God-given ability and education potential — has remained the same. "Guided Growth" has become its watchword.

Land for the school was secured in 1887, when William Muir (half brother of James Muir, a member of the original Salina Townsite Company,) sold 111 acres of farm land for $9168.75. Later that same year the Bishop of Kansas, The Right Reverend Thomas H. Vail laid the cornerstone of the main building, which was later to be known as Vail Hall. Construction began right away and by fall of 1888, students began arriving. There were only thirty-six pupils the first year, most of whom lived in town.

In Ruby Bramwell's history, *City on the Move — The Story of Salina*, it is said "Charles Seitz, who was to become closely associated with the school until the day of his death in 1962, recalled that on the first day he, his brother Theodore, and Charles Teague drove the two miles out from town in a two-wheeled cart." The enrollment more than doubled the following year. Today the campus accommodates two hundred cadets.

Bishop Thomas was president of the Board of Trustees until his death in 1895. He was also Rector of the school, except for a short period when Father Chittenden took over. When Thomas died, The Right Reverend Frank R. Millspaugh took an active interest in the school. In 1903, when the Missionary Diocese of Salina was formed, The Right Reverend Sheldon Griswold became involved, as would many of his successors. Among those with a keen interest in the institution was The Right Reverend Robert H. Mize, third bishop of the District, who as a priest served as Rector of St. John's from 1898 to 1905.

The growth of St. John's has been phenomenal. The success can be attributed to many fine people who devoted their whole lives to forming young men. Colonel W. L. Ganssle headed St. John's from 1915 to 1928; Colonel Roy W. Perkins who labored until his death in 1931; Newell A. Barker, a loyal senior master from 1917-1919; Colonel (and later "Father") Remy Clem, who died in 1990; and Colonel Keith G. Duckers, who has been at St. John's for over forty years, a long time member of the Cathedral, and one who has served on the vestry and also as mayor of Salina. The structural changes at St. John's have also been on a grand scale. When Vail Hall completely burned in 1978, it was replaced by the Vanier Academic Center (the Vaniers being a prominent Salina family and faithful members of the Cathedral,) new dormitories have been built (including one named for Bishop Mize,) a new middle school, a gymnasium and athletic center.

Cadets today come from all over the United States and several foreign countries. Board members include a number of Cathedral parishioners and the Dean, Father Richard Hatfield. Support for the institution comes from a variety of sources — for instance, The Mule-Skinners, an organization which contributes to scholarships for boys in need, set their goal at a half million dollars. The Cathedral itself has a scholarship, begun by Dean Frederic Litchman, and which is awarded annually to a worthy cadet.

Col. Keith G. Duckers, President, St. John's Military School.

The relationship between St. John's and Christ Cathedral has always been close and continues to grow stronger. Cadets march the two miles to the Cathedral several times a year to participate in Sunday liturgies with the Cathedral congregation. In 1991, the 103rd Corps was present for the dedication of new flag poles at the Cathedral, dedicated in honor of Col. Keith Duckers. The ceremony had extra meaning as the Gulf War in Iraq had just recently been successfully completed and the American flag was raised by war veteran Russell Kastner, nephew of parishioner Robert Kastner, who also

A large flag of the United States dominates the St. John's Military School campus. The Vanier Academic Center stands in the background.

served as Chairman of the Board at St. John's. In 1992, the 104th Corps, complete with brass band, attended Mass on a brisk Palm Sunday making for a grand palm procession.

The chaplain at St. John's is The Reverend Canon James R. Cox. Fr. Cox arrived at St. John's in 1990 after graduating from Nashotah House. He is a native of Garden City, Kansas, and a graduate of the University of Northern Colorado. He is a Regular Canon of Christ Cathedral. In his capacity as chaplain he celebrates daily Mass; teaches classes in religion and morals and ethics; and convenes the Chapel Council, a group of cadets who volunteer time to serve in the Chapel. Fr. Cox is also available to cadets as well as staff and families for counseling and spiritual guidance.

St. Barnabas Hospital, built at the instigation of Bishop Griswold, and completed in 1910. After St. Barnabas closed in 1922, it became the junior high school building at St. John's Military School.

Saint Barnabas Hospital

In the early 1900's, physicians in Salina maintained a hospital in a rented house in town. To say it was insufficient would be a gross understatement. In the Spring of 1909, a group of doctors approached The Right Reverend Sheldon Griswold and asked that the Church build a hospital. This he agreed to do, and at the Annual Men's Guild Dinner in May, he presented his plan to the Cathedral. Around the city, various civic groups pledged their support. Soon, trustees of St. John's Military School offered a site on their campus for the hospital. Bishop Griswold launched a campaign to raise funds. The final cost of building was $30,000. On October 25, 1910, St. Barnabas Hospital opened its doors. In Bramwell's book, there is an account of the event. She writes, "There was a reception and an address by Bishop Griswold. There were six cabs and three wagonettes engaged to convey the 200 people who attended." In addition to the money raised, a number of gifts were received to help in furnishing the offices, chapel, operating rooms and private rooms. Donations came from both church groups in Salina and other organizations in the region. Three months before the hospital opened, The Very Reverend William Masker, Dean of the Cathedral wrote to the congregation:

The fund for furnishing a room in St. Barnabas Hospital by the Cathedral parish amounts now to $52.63. The full amount needed is $100. As your Rector I took the responsibility of promising this amount to the Hospital for this purpose. I am not in the habit of making promises for the congregation. But having at the time no way of putting the matter before you, and feeling *that the matter is so much one of our Christian duty, I did so in this instance, trusting that you would sustain me. And the response already made assures me that you will. It is worth our notice that the parishes at Hutchinson and Minneapolis and the Missions at Kingman and WaKeeney have each pledged $100 for a room. Kingman has already paid in full.*

Soon after completion, the Board of Managers turned the administration of St. Barnabas over to Sister Mary Helena of the Sisters of Consolation. The hospital filled a need in Salina and was in constant use. The Sisters of Consolation asked to be relieved of the managerial duties in December, 1921. The hospital closed a year later and the land reverted to St. John's for use as a junior high school. The building was razed in 1965. Salina was not without health care, though; the Roman Catholic Church began St. John's Hospital in 1914, and the Methodist Church began work on Asbury Hospital in the early 1920's. The first real health care center in town though, owes its livelihood to Bishop Griswold, Dean Masker and the people of Christ Cathedral.

Saint Faith's House and the Deaconesses

The history of St. Faith's House and the history of deaconesses in Salina are inextricably woven. The small white frame building on North Ninth Street, across from Hawthorne School, was begun as a memorial to Mary Faith Hoag, infant daughter of The Very Reverend and Mrs. Victor Hoag, who died at three weeks old. Dean Hoag and men of the Cathedral parish constructed the building themselves in a six-week

The children who attended St. Faith's House pose following a weekday service.

period one hot Kansas summer.

Dean Hoag located the house in a section of town which at that time was alive with new homes, and where children of that area had no church school. With most building materials and labor furnished from within the parish, the cost of construction was minimal. Only the plastering and plumbing had to be paid for, and Cathedral members who could not donate labor or materials paid those expenses.

The communicants of Christ Cathedral viewed St. Faith's House as a local mission. There was not a lot of money to be spared, and the Cathedral had its financial responsibility to the National Church and its missionary work. With funds donated by the Hoags, which had been set aside by them for Mary Faith's college education, and local donations, the small mission opened its doors in the fall of 1922. Administration of St. Faith's House came under the auspices of the Missionary District, since the Salina congregation was too small and limited economically. The relationship remained friendly, and there was active cooperation between the Cathedral and St. Faith's.

The first paid worker was Miss Eleanor Ridgway, a UTO (United Thank Offering) worker, who arrived in Salina in 1923 and stayed until 1926. She lived in the back rooms of St. Faith's House and offered classes in religious education.

Deaconess Anne E. Gilliland arrived in Salina in 1926, and by 1927, the Salina superintendent of schools referred to St. Faith's House as "the most constructive piece of social work done in this city." Deaconess Gilliland instituted a library branch to make the checking out of books more convenient for the children of North Salina. In fact, the Salina Public Library provided her with $150 per year to purchase books for the branch. She started boys' and girls' clubs, sewing classes, story hours, mothers' club, as well as Sunday services, and Wednesday classes in religious instruction. She made visits to homes and provided counsel and concern for families living in the area of St. Faith's House.

The small frame building was enlarged during this time, adding a stage and classrooms. A small altar was placed in a room, creating a chapel, and baptisms and confirmations were conducted there. A guild of women confirmed at St. Faith's House began meeting and enlarging the work carried on there. Deaconess Anne Gulliland and St. Faith's became synonymous, and she was successful in enlisting the help of persons prominent in civic affairs.

The Order of Deaconesses was given canonical authority in 1889, after the Reverend William Reed Huntington petitioned the Church to revive the primitive order mentioned in the New Testament. A "set apart" status was provided for women who sought work in the social ministry of the Church. Generally college-educated, the women received further training provided by the National Church, and then were placed in areas of special needs, such as Appalachia or on Indian Reservations. The National Church provided the deaconesses with a yearly stipend and pension funds. The Order of Deaconesses was dissolved by the General Convention of 1970.

Deaconess Gilliland asked to retire in 1949 after twenty-three years of service to St. Faith's House. She remained a familiar sight in Salina, dressed in the garb of a deaconess, attending church functions until her death in 1958. She is memorialized by a stained glass window in St. Michael's Chapel at the Cathedral, given by the people of the parish.

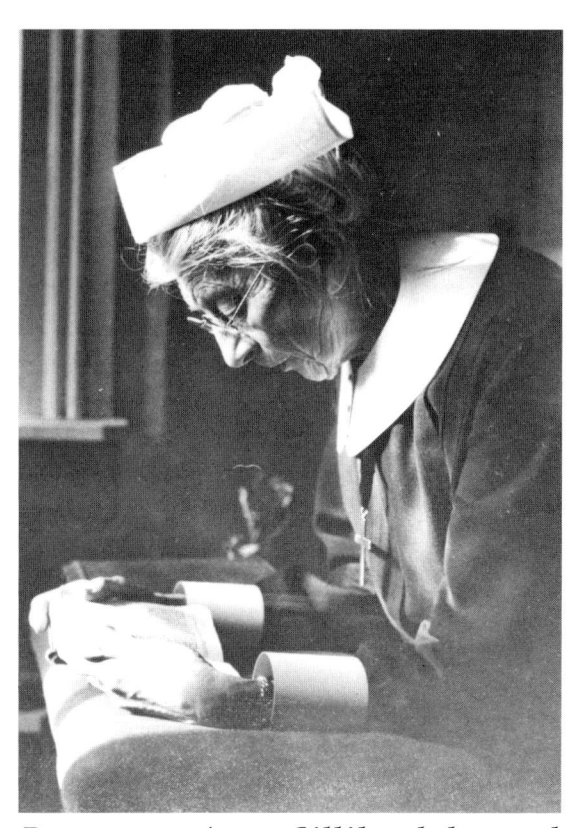

Deaconess Anne Gilliland devoted much of her life's work to St. Faith's House

Deaconess Evelyn Seymour, the last deaconess at St. Faith's House.

Deaconess Gilliland's successor was Evelyn Seymour, who served until 1958. By this time, social agencies in Salina had largely assumed many of the services performed in the classes at St. Faith's House. The zeal and mission of St. Faith's had peaked, and in spite of increased association with the Cathedral, the work of St. Faith's never achieved the intensity it had under the direction of Deaconess Gilliland. Deaconess Seymour left for work in an urban area, and Deaconess Eleanor Sime arrived to take her place.

With a change in bishops, the work of St. Faith's House became less clearly focused, and Deaconess Sime became disenchanted with her role in the Order of Deaconesses. She left the order in 1957, and Bishop Arnold Lewis made the decision to close the doors of St. Faith's House. Public outcry was to no avail — social work in the City of Salina had replaced the work done by St. Faith's, and funding had become a Cathedral responsibility, which it could ill-afford. Other religious institutions were functioning in the area, and the original need which was the basis for the founding of St. Faith's House, no longer existed.

The story of St. Faith's House ends where it began — with Father Hoag. From the Chapel of the Intercession of Trinity Parish, New York, he wrote to Salina in May, 1958:

I think that any mission station is stronger for being the little sister of some stronger parish nearby, and that the missionary understanding of any parish is sharpened by having an actual mission project all its own. At least in the case of the Cathedral congregation, which I found pauperized and ingrown, it got them over the hump. St. Faith's taught them outreach and concern."

He added, "It was based on the pattern of mission stations in the form of house with chapel attached. I celebrated at the little altar there one morning each week. A resident woman worker was on hand constantly at all hours, for friendly contacts and services to the community... starting with the children.

That's what St. Faith's was all about. It served its purpose.

Saint Francis Boys' Home / The Saint Francis Academy

Like St. John's Military School, St. Francis Academy is an Episcopal institution, based in Salina and known around the country for its work with troubled youth. The founder of St. Francis was The Right Reverend Robert H. Mize, son of Bishop Mize of the Missionary District.

Canon Kenneth Yates, Bishop Robert "Fr. Bob" Mize and Canon Phillip Rapp of St. Francis Academy, 1990.

"Father Bob" as he is still known, working with his father at St. John's in the 1940's, perceived a need for a home for boys whose parents could not afford to send them to the Military School. In his missionary work around Western Kansas, he found boys in dire need of discipline and Christian training.

Father Bob's vision for a place to help such boys got off the ground in September, 1945, when he leased the Ellsworth County Poor Farm and moved in with about a dozen boys, much to the displeasure of the local citizens. That same year, the first Saint Francis Boy's Home was incorporated. The idea was great, but putting his plans into action took a while. The Reverend Canon William Craig, successor to Mize and an honorary canon of Christ Cathedral, recounts the early days of the Boys' Home:

The first three years were chaos. He [Fr. Bob] took in every kid who came along, regardless of age, background, psychological problems or not, delinquent, dependent, neglected, all in a 'mix'. And, as he has told me, every boy ran away at least once, and a number of boys ran away three, four, or five times. Usually when a boy runs away, he steals a car locally, and we bought a lot of cars in those days that boys had stolen and wrecked. I'm always amazed that Ellsworth, which is not a big place, had enough cars to go around!

In the beginning, survival was hand to mouth; Fr. Bob and the boys lived off donations from farmers and what they could produce themselves. Support was not long in coming though; a Board of Trustees, the Diocese and the Kansas Department of Social Welfare all became involved. Fr. Bob overcame a mistrust of psychologists and social workers and eventually a whole staff joined together, keeping in mind the motto of the founder, "Therapy in Christ".

Discipline, therapy, forgiveness and Christian love have long been the mainstays of working with the boys. Daily

Residents of St. Francis, working on the farm.

"Father Bob's boys" line up in front of the Ellsworth unit of St. Francis Boy's Home.

prayer (at one time daily Mass) integration in local schools and involvement in the community have all been ingredients in the healing process. The "success" rate is staggering; while not all the boys have been set straight, many have gone on to be successful businessmen, husbands, fathers and even priests. From Emily Gardiner Neal's book, *Bob and His Boys*, the essence of St. Francis is discovered:

> *Father Bob always intended to make a real home for his boys; he was determined that it should be neither a reformatory nor a large and impersonal 'Children's Home' full of regimented youngsters segregated from the rest of society. His success was apparent when St. Francis' old boys began flocking back, usually unannounced, with such explanations as, 'I wanted to come home for Thanksgiving,' or 'I came to spend my vacation with my family'.*

Fr. Bob left in 1960 on a sabbatical to South Africa, having not had a vacation in fifteen years. While engaged in youth work for the Archbishop there, he was elected Bishop of Damaraland, a diocese in Southwest Africa. He later returned to the United States and now lives in California. His successor was Fr. Craig, who was appointed President and CEO in 1961. Twenty years later, he was followed by The Reverend Kenneth Yates, one-time development director of Nashotah House and a canon of Christ Cathedral. The current leader of St. Francis is The Reverend Canon Phillip J. Rapp, also a canon of the Cathedral.

St. Francis facilities and population have expanded over time. In addition to the home at Ellsworth, a second home was begun at Bavaria, outside of Salina. National headquarters were established on East Elm Street in Salina in 1960. A treatment unit was opened in Lake Placid, New York, in 1965; an early-intervention program, called Passport for Adventure, was established in Kansas; an outpatient program called Adirondack Experience was begun in New York in 1990; and recently St. Francis began work with the St. Michael's Home in Picayune, Mississippi (the priest in that facility is The Reverend Jay Breisch, an Honorary Canon of Christ Cathedral.) In 1990, the name was officially changed to The Saint Francis Academy Incorporated. St. Francis is accredited by various health care agencies and is licensed to treat a wide variety of disorders. Research indicates a success rate over 70%, which in one of the highest in the country.

Ties to the local church have been an important aspect in the treatment of the residents since its founding. As an incentive for good behavior, boys would be awarded membership at St. Francis. Neal's book relates the story of the ceremony in 1950:

> *The choir stalls of Christ*

Cathedral in Salina were filled that night with fifty St. Francis boys. Sitting near the altar the Bishop of Salina admitted twenty-one boys to be members of St. Francis; and three were admitted to be honorary members... Two boys, one from Ellsworth and one from Bavaria, said Evening Prayer before admission. No rehearsal had been necessary; their clear young voices carried throughout the cathedral building as easily as they did in their small chapels at the Homes... Father Bob presented the candidates to the Bishop by saying, 'I present unto you these persons to be received as Members in the fellowship and fraternity of the St. Francis Boys' Homes.' One by one, they came: Joe, the formerly expert car stealer; Frank, the ex-arsonist; Tim, the sometime robber.

To this date, St. Francis residents continue to attend the Cathedral on Sunday mornings, often times serving as acolytes. In November, 1990, there was a celebration at the Cathedral to commemorate forty-five years of service, to recognize the new ministry of Fr. Rapp and to inaugurate the new name. Bishop Mize traveled to Salina for the event and participated in the Mass along with Bishops William Davidson and John Ashby. A dinner followed at the Salina Country Club at which Bishop Mize gave an inspiring account of his years of work.

The Ashby House

The stately home at 150 South Eighth Street, just south of the Cathedral, which once served as home to the Cathedral deans, is now a shelter for homeless families. When the deans stopped living in the house, the structure was given over to the Diocese and served for a while as a halfway house. When it was time for a new lease to be issued, a group from the Cathedral spearheaded a move to have the building used for outreach to families in need. In 1991, approval was won from The Right Reverend John Ashby to use the house in a new capacity. Barbara Young and Sara Osborn, parishioners of Christ Cathedral, began forming a plan to provide housing and assistance to impoverished families. Salina already had provisions for single men or women, but not families. The goal in revitalizing the house was to offer room and board and provide the skills needed for a family to get a fresh start. Unlike other places, the purpose was not merely to be a transient shelter.

With an unsettled economy, many people had been finding themselves unable to hold jobs or pay bills. The goal of Ashby House has been to extend a roof over the head and put food on the table for up to thirty days. At the same time, trained counselors are to offer

The former Deanery in its latest role as Ashby House, a shelter for homeless families, 150 South Eighth Street.

assistance in life skills, including educational planning, personal health and hygiene, financial management and time organization. Support groups and referral services can also be networked through Ashby House.

The home was cleaned, refurbished, modernized and set up to accommodate as many as forty-eight destitute families a year. Members of the Cathedral, as well as other churches in the area, volunteered time, donated many items, (including money), and got the House opened in early 1992. It has been at near capacity most of the time since then. Dean Hatfield serves as Chairman of the Board of Trustees and Bishop Ashby is an ex-officio member of the Board.

Christ Cathedral has always been involved in the community in many ways. Canned food drives, such as the "Souper Bowl" and collecting articles for the Emergency Aid / Food Bank are just two ongoing examples of such desire to help. Offerings are regularly collected for clergy discretionary funds. During Lent, donations are set aside for special purposes outside the local area — the 1992 offering went for the training of priests in the Province of Papau, New Guinea. Concern for those outside the local family will always be a priority for a Christian community, such as Christ Cathedral.

VIII. Inside the Walls

What then is Apollos? What is Paul? Servants through whom you believed, as the Lord assigned to each. I planted, Apollos watered, but God gave the growth. So neither he who plants nor he who waters is anything, but only God who gives the growth. He who plants and he who waters are equal, and each shall receive his wages according to his labor. For we are God's fellow workers; you are God's field, God's building. According to the grace of God given to me, like a skilled master builder I laid a foundation, and another man is building upon it. Let each man take care how he builds upon it. For no other foundation can any one lay than that which is laid, which is Jesus Christ. — 1 Corinthians 3:5-11

Christian Education

A major emphasis at Christ Cathedral from the time of her construction has been the education and formation of the faithful. Bishops, clergy and people alike have spoken over the years on the necessity of a solid program of teaching, especially for young people. The programs have taken different directions over time, but with a single goal always in mind — to come to more fully understand the faith of Christ. The variety of styles over the years has simply been the result of a turnover in directors, teachers, curriculum, accommodations and scheduling.

Sunday School has been taught regularly since the early days of the Church in Salina. The hours have changed from one era to the next; classes have been held, before, in between and after Sunday services. There have even been occasions when Sunday School was held in the middle of the week. The latest program has classes for forty five minutes between the early and late Mass on Sundays during the school year, for kindergarten through high school age students. Christ Cathedral is in the process of writing its own new Sunday School curriculum based on the liturgical year. The lessons, which are adjusted for different age levels, are rooted in Scripture and traditional Church teaching. Various art and craft projects accompany the lessons. Of course, none of the work would be possible without the dedication and commitment of the many people who have taught Sunday School over the years.

A new part of the education program is the Adult Forum. Each Sunday at 9:00, while the young people run off to Sunday School, an adult group gathers in the parish hall. The topic of discussion

Saint Lucia (Sophia Osborn) visits Sunday School students.

varies from year to year, but the goal is always to educate and make the faith a viable and strong part of a person's life. Church history, prayer and liturgy are often used to focus the sessions.

The education program at any church should be of the utmost importance; this is especially so at a cathedral, which should set an example for the entire diocese. At Christ Cathedral, the chances to learn have been plentiful. From clubs which formed to study Scripture, to youth groups, to the time when deaconesses concentrated on teaching, many opportunities have been available. Christian formation of course, extends beyond the classroom on a Sunday morning; Bible Study, Confirmation Class (Inquirer's Class), Vacation Bible School, Lenten classes and church camp are just a few exam-

A newly-formed Boys' Choir poses with clergy and layservers of Christ Cathedral, 1920.

ples of what Christ Cathedral has offered over the years.

Music

Music at Christ Cathedral has always played an integral part in the service of worship. It provides a universal language through which the entire congregation praises God, either vocally or instrumentally. Throughout the years, a host of musicians from around the world have offered many beautiful sounds inside Salina's Early-Gothic Cathedral.

The original organ was dedicated on Ascension Day, 1908, with an evening recital played by Mr. Roland Diggle from St. John's Church in Wichita. A gift from Mrs. Sarah E. Batterson, magnanimous benefactress of the Cathedral, the first organ was ordered and installed by the House of Pilcher. Grace Wellington, organist and choir director in the old Christ Church, continued her work at the Cathedral. During 1909, Canon George B. Kinkead engaged Frederick Rocke from Ireland to fill the post of organist and choir director.

In 1910, Arthur Davis, a fellow of the Royal College of Organists, supervised the formation of the Boys' Choir. Most of the boys were cadets from St. John's Military School, but boys were recruited from Salina as well. They were paid fifty cents per month for performance and rehearsals, with a five cent penalty for missing rehearsals. The practice of paying choir members for performances and rehearsals continued well into the 1930's.

Edward Kimball was a member of the Boys' Choir, and in his auto-biographical notes remembered that he was a "professional boy soprano." He added that on Sunday mornings he first attended the Presbyterian Church, and then went to the Cathedral for performance with the choir, since his family thought it "safe to participate in a high rite thereafter." He recalled also, "liking the theatrical trappings' and the "entrances and exits made with angelic solemnity."

Several musicians held the post of organist in the early days, including Miss Katherine Eberhardt, Miss Margaret Utt, Mrs. Frank Green, a Miss Bradley and a Mr. Hulburt. In 1918, George W. Barnes

An electronic mechanism can be seen from inside the bell tower, which is connected to a console inside the cathedral.

accompanied The Reverend John C. Sage, newly-elected Bishop of The Missionary District to Salina, to serve at the Cathedral.

Mr. Banes, besides his duties as organist and choirmaster at the Cathedral, taught vocal music at Washington High School and conducted the Salina Oratorio Society. He was designated Visiting Choirmaster at other churches in Salina, including St. John's Lutheran, First Presbyterian and First Christian Church.

In the fall of 1921, Edward Ritchings held the organist's position at the Cathedral. He was the youngest member ever admitted to the Royal College of Organists, and as a member of Salina's Lion's Club, composed a marching song for that organization.

The relationship between the Cathedral and St. John's Military School provided a long list of organists and choir directors, as well as voices for the choir. When transportation for the cadets became a problem, members of the congregation formed a permanent choir. Later on, parish members such as Frances Baxter and Mrs. Jack Horner filled the void of organists. Royce Young, member of the American Guild of Organists, was appointed organist in 1973, and holds the position today. Mr. Young also teaches choral and instrumental music in the Salina school system.

The set of chime bells were regularly heard in Salina. From 1923 to 1925, Ernest Smith, a member of the Boys' Choir, played the chimes twice daily — fifteen minutes at noon and the Angelus at 6:00 pm. The bells are still played at special occasions such as weddings, funerals, and church celebrations. Until the bells were electrified in 1966, and could be played by a console placed near the organ, teams of men or boys had to pull on long ropes hanging from each bell. Later, a console of levers was installed in the bell tower, still requiring much physical effort. In the 1950's, Carl Hempsted transposed nearly 150 hymns and played the bells in the late afternoons as Salinans left work. It was during this time that Mrs. Bea Hempsted directed the choir.

The great tenor bell was used to call the congregation to worship. It was played by the Dean or an eager child, pulling on a long rope which hung in the nave. Now this bell can be played by flicking a switch in the Sacristy.

A later addition to the music department of the Cathedral has been the formation of a hand bell choir, featuring a set of forty-three bells reaching three and a half octaves. Called St. Cecilia's Bell Choir, the players begin at about age ten and Royce Young is their teacher and director. The bells were an anonymous gift to the music department of the church in 1976. The ten to fifteen students of the hand bell program perform regularly at the Sunday liturgies.

Care and maintenance of the original organ had been pushed beyond its capabilities, and in 1977 the cathedral parishioners undertook the purchase and installation of a new instrument. The new Cathedral organ features a console designed to be moved to the center of the chancel for recitals. This feature was most appreciated when local and area organists performed a Bach recital on the occasion of that composer's 300th anniversary of his birth in 1985. The organ also plays an integral part in local hymn-sings, Advent lessons and carols, as well as regular liturgies.

Today, Mrs. Shelley Hatfield conducts the Cathedral Choir, and music has once again become a prominent part of worship. As the Choir has become known for its superb quality, requests have come from parishes in Dodge City and Concordia for help. In 1990, the Choir traveled to Norton, Kansas to sing for a Solemn High Mass. The Children's Choir of Christ Cathedral has also gone on the road, performing in Larned, Kansas in 1991. Other instruments and groups are often heard in the Cathedral, including bagpipes, string quartet, brass groups, voices and instruments, all raising many a joyful noise unto the Lord.

St. Cecilia's Bell Choir.

The second organ at Christ Cathedral, a Moeller, new in 1977.

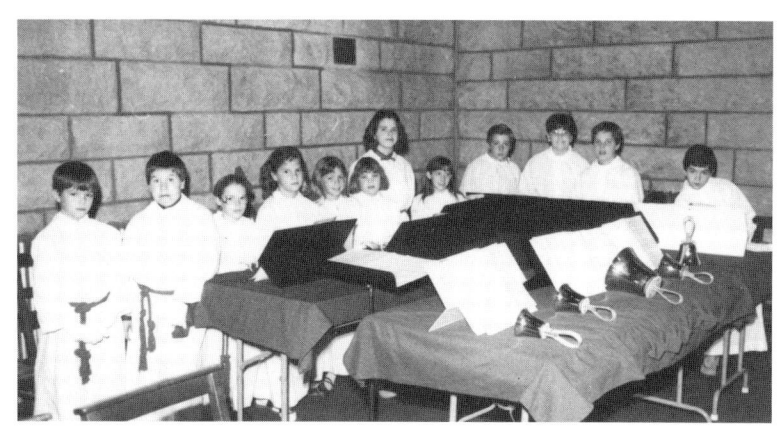

Women of the Church

Earliest records of activities related to the women of the church indicate that a chapter of the order, Daughters of the King, was established in 1885. Their purpose was one of "desiring to dedicate themselves to the life of prayer and service for the spread of Christ's Kingdom." Throughout the years, the Cathedral women have been doing just that, as well as some more mundane activities to generate monies for needed expenses.

In 1893, mention is made of the women referring to themselves as the Bishop Vail Branch of the Daughters of the King. The Right Reverend Thomas H. Vail was the first bishop of Kansas, before the diocese was split in half. The women of Christ Church assessed monthly dues of ten cents from their eighteen members. After accumulating $110, the women gave their money to the church for stained glass windows and their installation.

A Christmas bazaar of 1893 netted $42.10, and this money was given to the vestry to pay a lumber and light bill. In September, 1894, the women adopted a "Blue Bag" system of collecting money, which was the forerunner of the United Thank Offering.

In 1896, the women donated $18 for the purchase of prayerbooks and hymnals. At Easter of that year, in an annual report, the treasurer gave the following account: "$99.55 cash received; $99.76 cash paid; leaving the treasury quite empty."

During the rest of the 1890's, the women held dinners, bazaars, phonograph socials, or other fund-raising events, always using their profits for church expenses. At one point they purchased altar vases; another time they paid for repairs for the stove used to heat the church. The women also attended study groups, such as the one where Mrs. De Longy, the rector's wife, presented a paper on hymns of the church. At a later meeting, the rector gave a series of talks on church history while the women sewed.

Christian outreach was a concern of these early groups of women, and records show that they collected boxes of clothing for Indian missions in Nebraska and South Dakota. They also provided necessities for needy children in Salina, and baked breads and made jellies for Christ Hospital in Topeka.

Soon after the Missionary District of Salina was formed, the Daughters of the King were apparently disbanded and replaced by the Women's Auxiliary. Few records survive these years of Cathedral construction, but it is known that for years the Women's Auxiliary served chicken noodle dinners to the Lions Club, for twenty-five cents each.

This money accumulated until enough was on hand to purchase the two of the five stained-glass windows in the wall back of the high altar. These were among the first stained-glass windows placed in the Cathedral.

In the years that followed, certain factors worked against a formal organization for the women of the church. Certain bishops or deans declared it unseemly that women should be actively involved with fund-raising for church expenses. World War I and the influenza epidemic that followed curtailed meetings and programs. The Great Depression had a definite effect on all areas of life, and the women of the church were not immune to national distress.

In the late 1930's, Dean Hewitt B. Vinnedge asked that the women meet to organize into circles. He probably intended for study or service groups to emerge from this, but according to Nell Wood, a 55 year church member, the women who joined the circles decided to hostess twice-monthly bridge sessions at a cost of twenty-five cents each, and that money was turned over to the church's general fund. A second World War interrupted the bridge sessions, and under Dean James T. Golder's wife, Helen, an altar guild was started, supplanting any organized women's groups.

When Dean Frederic Litchman arrived in 1947, the women of the church were organized into three guilds — St. Martha's, St. Elizabeth's, and St. Anne's. An organ repair bill of $10,000 was reason enough to once again begin the bazaar business, and the Christmas bazaars prepared by the Women of Christ Cathedral became a Salina tradition. More money was generated when the women decided on a second bazaar in the spring — a patio bazaar featuring homemade items for outdoor use. A thrift shop was opened in the former bishop's house, staffed entirely by volunteer women. Cookbooks were compiled and sold, proof that the women of Christ Cathedral were "the best cooks in town."

With the construction of the new parish house completed in 1948, the women sold light bulbs, in cooperation with Kansas Power and Light, and with that money supplied the kitchen with stoves and other needed items. During the 1950's and 1960's the women of the church paid for items needed by the altar guild, and each of the guilds began study programs, particularly in seasons of Lent or Advent. Sewing groups were established, and from these came the needlepoint work that added to the beauty of the Cathedral. In 1968, all guilds cooperated for a "Tasting Tea" for the benefit of St. Francis Boys' Homes.

Social changes of the 1970's affected the Women of the Church, now called Episcopal Church Women. As more women entered the workforce, they had less time for the social, study and service programs in formal organizations. Fewer numbers resulted in general decline of major projects, yet those women who remained have been faithful to the United Thank Offering, rummage sales, parish dinners, fund-raisers for kitchen remodeling, donations to Boy Scout Troop #1, Camp PECUSA, and St. Francis Academy. Study groups were offered in the evenings, as well as daytime. Food is supplied to parish families at the time of death; lap robes are made for nursing homes; cards are mailed to hospitalized church members. A remnant of St. Elizabeth's guild still meets weekly to help with the mailing of *The Cathedral Times.*

The contributions of the women of Christ Cathedral have been many and varied, and continue to be so today. Perhaps the afternoon teas and phonograph socials have been replaced by a core of women who can organize a reception for a visiting bishop over the telephone, but the women of the church remain a valuable resource.

Altar Guild

Reflecting the nature of its work, there is no definitive record of the work of the Altar guild at Christ Cathedral. Like the hundreds of women who have quietly gone about their duties, there is no self-aggrandizing account of their contributions to the work in the sacristy.

There would not have been a sacristy in Watson's general mercantile store in 1870, where the first Salina Episcopalians met, nor would there have been treasured vessels, linens or vestments to care for. Perhaps a frontier woman provided a cloth for the impoverished altar, and maybe even homemade bread and wine.

Christ Cathedral now has four indoor altars, each kept in immaculate condition by the Altar Guild. They work with "Martha" hands and "Mary" hearts, as they polish candelabra or tend to the gold service, set with the jewels from Mrs. Sarah Batterson. Some members today were trained for their work by Mrs. Virginia Rose; some members today are daughters of former Altar Guild members, carrying on family traditions of sacristy service.

Older Altar Guild members can remember the hardships of carrying water from the women's lavatory to be heated on a one-burner hot plate. Others remember several seasons of Holy Lent, when Altar Guild members met to sew linens, carefully using twenty tiny stitches to an inch. Prior to Holy Week, Altar Guild members still meet to create small crosses to be given to communicants on Palm Sunday.

Sometimes former members' talents are called upon. Mrs. Emily Cheney, an excellent needleworker, was asked to repair a lovely, but aged, lace frontal, saving it from destruction. It is still in use today at the High Altar.

Altar Guild duty today is not without its moments of anxiety. One remembers the time a worker entered the Chapel, and was shocked to find a man asleep atop the altar. She excitedly ran to Dean Litchman to exclaim, "A man is sleeping on top the altar and has taken everything off." The Dean was relieved to find the local character had "taken off" only the linens, and was not sleeping nude. Thereafter, the doors of the Cathedral were locked, and Altar Guild members were issued keys.

The Altar Guild was named St. Anne's Altar Guild with the arrival of Dean Hatfield, and each member was given a medal of St. Anne to wear. Directoresses now serve terms of approximately one year, rotating the duties of scheduling and calling meetings of the entire guild. At this time, Babette Freeman is Directoress, and her predecessors include Nancy Bressler and Donna Vanier.

Aside from times when the Altar Guild meets as a group, the teams assigned to specific weeks quietly go about their duties. They continue the work of those women who have served before them, polishing cruets, washing, ironing, preparing the vessels, laying out vestments, and taking special care of the Cathedral's beautiful treasures.

Boy Scout Troop Number 1

For many years, Christ Cathedral has had the distinct honor of sponsoring Boy Scout Troop #1. Whether this troop was the first Boy Scout troop organized in the United States cannot be proven or disproved. However, several facts attest to the plausibility of such a claim.

It is known that Francis John Romanes and Lloyd Holsapple both attended Oxford University in England with Sir Robert Baden-Powell, who started the Scout movement in the British Isles. Mr. Romanes, who had served in the British Army and had seen action in the Sudan, was persuaded by Bishop Sheldon M. Griswold to come to Salina as an instructor at St. John's Military School. The Reverend Lloyd Holsapple, a Canon at Christ Cathedral, was conducting missions in the area.

At the Christmas Day liturgy in 1909, the first vested boys' choir presented its first musical offering, and as a reward and incentive to continue in the choir, Mr. Romanes began instructing the boys in the ways of scouting, according to the British model. Earlier, Mr. Romanes had written in his journal of December 13, "Have implanted the germ of Boy Scouting firmly among several boys, I think." In January, 1910, he would further add, "Patrol definitely formed."

Meetings were held in the guild house, and the boys named themselves the Raven Patrol. Those first members were Walter Eitel, Raymond Fenn, John Fuller, Louis Gottschick, DeWitt Holloway, Arthur Hurlburg, Lloyd Livingstone, William Mitchell, Leslie Wilson and William Zeising.

The Raven uniform consisted of a blue shirt, khaki pants buttoned just below the knee, black neckerchief with a white border. Each boy carried a knife, a whistle and a stave. For hikes and camping, a knapsack was added. In the summer of 1910, the fledgling Scouts held their first camp on the John Markey ranch, near Bennington.

That same year, the Wolf Patrol was formed, in which the boys wore neckerchiefs with orange borders to distinguish themselves from the Raven Patrol. A few months later, a third patrol was formed, calling themselves the Eagles.

In the spring of 1910, Mr. Romanes left Salina for Denver to become Scout Commissioner for the Denver area. The Boy Scouts of America were incorporated in February, 1910, but it was not until December, 1910, that National Headquarters had any record of troops formed in Kansas, fully a year after the program started by Mr. Romanes at Christ Cathedral, Salina.

Canon Holsapple continued as Scoutmaster, assisted by Dean George Kinkead, and Earl Griffith. Dr. H.N. Moses instructed the Scouts in first aid, and Dr. Moses later said, "The outstanding feature of the Salina Scouts is that they were organized by a British Boy Scout officer who received his training under Sir Baden-Powell," the founder of the movement.

The intervention of two world wars weakened the interest in Scouting at the Cathedral. It was not until June, 1949, that the Cathedral Vestry voted that a Boy Scout troop be sponsored. Due to strong activity at the Air Force base, a Boy Scout Charter was received in November, 1949, and the troop once again became active. With the closing of the base, interest again waned, and the troop stopped meeting.

In 1976, Ashley Null, Eagle Scout and communicant of the Cathedral, began a movement to bring Troop #1

Members of Raven Patrol, Boy Scout Troop #1, with Dean Kinkead.

back to life. His efforts were a race against time, as the deadline for re-establishing Troop #1 was fast approaching. Unless he could organize the required personnel and paperwork in timely fashion, Troop #1 would be officially disbanded and no new troop could ever bear its name or number.

With the help of Cathedral member Harvey Hoover, Ashley, and Scott Fosbinder, another Cathedral communicant and Scout, found the necessary number of Scouts to belong to the troop. On February 28, 1977, Ashley Null presented the necessary documents to Rod Huddleston, Three Rivers District Scout Executive of the Coronado Area Council, and the Raven Patrol, Troop #1 of Christ Cathedral was saved from extinction.

Since then, the troop has steadily grown and owes its survival to Ashley Null, now an ordained priest of the Church and currently studying in Cambridge, his father, Dr. W.G. Null, Harvey Hoover, Mike Hitchcock, Jack Lambert, and many others, all of whom provided much-needed leadership as the troop re-established itself. One of the on-going traditions carried out by Troop #1 is the Shrove Tuesday pancake supper prepared each year at the Cathedral.

The last two ceremonies conferring the titles of Eagle Scout to members of Troop #1 were for David Litchman and Pieter Miller. David is the step-son of Scoutmaster Jack Lambert, and grandson of the late Dean, Frederic W. Litchman. Pieter is the son of assistant Scoutmaster, Doug Miller. Their receiving this hard-earned honor indicates that the spirit of Boy Scouting continues to thrive at Christ Cathedral.

IX. The Later Days

Then I saw a new heaven and a new earth; for the first heaven and the first earth had passed away, and the sea was no more. And I saw the holy city, new Jerusalem, coming down out of heaven from God, prepared as a bride adorned for her husband; and I heard a loud voice from the throne saying, "Behold, the dwelling of God is with men. He will dwell with them, and they shall be his people, and God himself will be with them; he will wipe away every tear from their eyes, and death shall be no more, neither shall there be mourning nor crying nor pain any more, for the former things have passed away." And he who sat upon the throne said, "Behold, I make all things new." Also he said, "Write this, for these words are trustworthy and true." And he said to me, "It is done! I am the Alpha and the Omega, the beginning and the end. To the thirsty I will give from the fountain of the water of life without payment. He who conquers shall have this heritage, and I will be his God and he shall be my son.
— Revelation 21:2-7

From the earliest days of the Church, Christians have always gathered together to celebrate the sacraments and to enjoy fellowship. From the quaint countrysides of England to the bustling cities of Europe, cathedrals have always been at the center of this life. While Salina is thousands of miles from Salisbury, Chartres, or Colonge — Christ Cathedral stands with those majestic buildings, beckoning the faithful.

Like her sister cathedrals around the world, there is so much that makes up the history of Christ Cathedral, that one scarcely knows where to start, let alone end. From the people, to the buildings, to the programs, the story of Christ Cathedral encompasses many parts of life. One would be remiss to ignore those events which fall between chapters, especially those things which have taken place in recent history. So what follows then, in no particular order, are just more parts of the story.

Father Willys Neustrom during the construction of the outdoor Stations of the Cross, 1991.

Fr. Kimmett blesses the statue of the Blessed Virgin at the dedication of the outdoor Stations of the Cross, with Fr. Neustrom at the left, and Fathers Cox, Hatfield and Wells to the right.

Stations of the Cross

In the area south of the education building is a quiet place called the Cathedral Park, complete with a gazebo. An outstanding feature was added to the park in 1991, when The Reverend Willys E. Neustrom, a long-time priest of the Diocese and associate of the Cathedral, created outdoor Stations of the Cross. In his retirement, Fr. Neustrom spent many months hand carving and piecing together the stations from red cedar, walnut, gold leaf and copper. The Stations sit along a cross-shaped walk way and are lit at night. Landscaping has added to the beauty of the setting. The space also serves as an outdoor columbarium. The Stations were the gift of Fr. and Mrs.

Neustrom. They were dedicated on St. Michael's Day, 1991, only a few hours before Mrs. Gerri Neustrom died, following a long illness. The Stations have been heavily traveled by pilgrims from all around the region; young children and visiting Sunday Schools have reverently walked the Way of the Cross, parishioners in Lent have corporately prayed outdoors, and following a front-page article in The Salina Journal on Good Friday, 1992, hundreds of people flocked to the Park to make devotions.

Visitors and Guests

Since the arrival of Fr. Hatfield in 1988, the Cathedral has been privileged to host many dignitaries from around the world. With his South Africa connections, the Dean arranged for four different bishops from that Province to visit the Cathedral; The Right Reverend Derek G. Damant, Bishop of George; The Right Reverend Sigisbert Ndwandwe, Suffragan of Johannesburg; The Right Reverend Thomas S. Stanage, Bishop of Bloemfontein; and The Right Reverend Patrick Matalengwe, sometime Suffragan of Cape Town and now Dean of All Saints' Cathedral, Milwaukee, Wisconsin. Salina has become a popular stopping point, not only for world travelers, but for other visitors as well, in particular, Sisters of the Convent of the Holy Nativity in Fond du Lac, Wisconsin. Preaching, teaching, leading workshops and quiet days, the nuns are always anxious to visit Christ Cathedral.

In 1991, the Cathedral hosted the Diocesan Convention, at which the Presiding Bishop was guest preacher. On the last Sunday before Lent, 1992, Archmandrite Basil Essey, Dean of Saint

Dean Richard Hatfield and visiting South African Bishop Thomas Stanage, 1990.

George Orthodox Cathedral in Wichita was the guest preacher at Evensong. Two months later, a contingent from Christ Cathedral made a reciprocal visit to St. George for a Lenten liturgy and dinner. Father Essey was consecrated auxiliary bishop for the Antiochian Archdiocese of North America in May, 1992. Among other visitors to the Cathedral in 1992, was Dr. Cynthia Campbell, pastor of First Presbyterian Church in Salina — at the time the largest Presbyterian congregation in the country to be led by a woman. She was the preacher at Mass on the Assumption, addressing the congregation on the ecumenical nature of Mary.

Relations with those outside the Anglican Communion has been an important feature at Christ Cathedral in recent years. Typifying this outlook, The Right Reverend Monsignor Raymond Menard, of the Roman Catholic Diocese of Salina, was made an Honorary Canon of the Cathedral. He is

Roman Catholic Bishop George Fitzsimons, with the Right Reverend John Ashby, Bishop of Western Kansas, 1992.

the first Roman monsignor to receive such an honor anywhere in the United States. Menard, a long-time friend of the Cathedral, first preached at Evensong in the 1950's, at the invitation of Dean Litchman. Menard has himself been involved in ecumenical relations during his years in Salina. News of his "canonization by the Episcopal Church", as the event was jokingly referred to, made the front page of both The Salina Journal and The Northwestern Kansas Register. In The Register article, Menard's letter of acceptance was quoted:

I am delighted to accept the honor that you have so graciously extended to me. It will be my delight to be with you and the clerics of the Episcopal community in Salina accompanied by some members of the Roman Catholic persuasion on the Eve of the Annunciation. I look upon the honor of becoming an Honorary Canon as a continuing ecumenical interest of our persuasions in Kansas.

Among those participating in the Seating of Canons on March 24, 1992, was the Roman Bishop, The Most Reverend George Fitzsimons. Other Cathedral Canons seated on the occasion were The Reverend Joseph M. Kimmett, curate; The Reverend James R. Cox, chaplain at St. John's; and The Reverend Philip J. Rapp, CEO at St. Francis.

Parish Life

One of the basics of church life, all over the world is the parish dinner. Whether it be a fund raiser for the women, pancakes served by the Boy Scouts, or a potluck, sharing a meal together is an important thing for Christians to do. Suppers at Christ Cathedral have always been emphasized; in recent years they have been scheduled on holy days to encourage Mass attendance.

Clergy prepare a meal (l to r) Frs. Kimmett, Cox, Neustrom, Hatfield, Bishop Ashby, Fr. Litchman.

The Presentation in February, The Feast of St. Mary in August and All Saints in November, are just a few examples of the parish gathering to eat. In addition, near the Feast of the Epiphany in January, a Twelfth Night celebration, complete with a Sunday School Christmas pageant, has become popular. The Seder dinner in Holy Week, which recalls the Passover Jesus ate before his Passion, is another mainstay, always packed to capacity. Another favorite among Cathedral parishioners are "Friday nights in Lent", to which everyone brings a covered dish to pass, before going on to the Stations of the Cross, a meditation and Benediction. A new event which has quickly gained popularity is the Pentecost Fete. The Whitsunday festivities include special foods, crafts, games and races; all to make money for special Cathedral programs.

The Youth

The involvement of the young people in parish life is absolutely essential. So often Episcopalians will talk about the need for ministries for the youth, "because they are the Church of tomorrow." Such statements are only half right; ministry to young people is important, but it is because they are already part of the Church, today! Involving the youth in the liturgies as acolytes and choir members is one way of showing them that they are needed members of the community. Sunday School and Youth Group are other means of involving the younger people.

A new plan at Christ Cathedral calls for the Sunday School students to paint Bible scenes on the walls of the education building, thereby giving them a sense of pride and ownership. The Youth Group meanwhile gathers middle and high school students together for extra activities. Since Fr. Joseph Kimmett took charge of youth work, the focus has been on forming a group which will pray together, play together, work together and study together. Some meetings are serious and others are just for fun. In the Spring of 1992, the youth group toured Salina by night; they visited places that are open twenty four hours a day to observe (in the words of a collect for night time) "those who work, while others sleep." After traveling the city most of the night, the group eventually crawled into sleeping bags on the parish hall floor.

One aspect of youth ministry in the Diocese of Western Kansas in which the Cathedral has been involved, is Teens Encounter Christ (TEC). It is a program which runs several times a year around the Diocese, for three days at a time. It

Youth and clergy from Western Kansas attend Camp Ilium in Colorado.

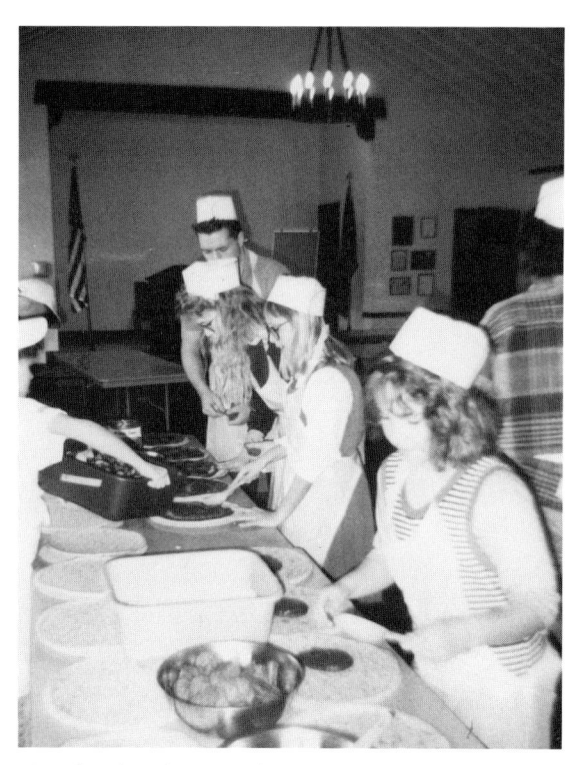

Cathedral youth prepare pizzas as part of a fund-raising project.

is geared to bring high school students into a closer relationship with God. The Cathedral hosted TEC just after Easter in 1991. Later that year, Father Hatfield served as spiritual director for a weekend in Hutchinson. Two Cathedral families have been very involved and supportive of this activity; the Kruckemyers and Wilburs.

Brian Kruckemyer and Lee Wilbur have each been in charge of one of the weekends, and have also been part of the Diocesan [Youth] Leadership Team.

The Office

In terms of administration, Christ Cathedral continues to move forward and grow. In the office, the position of secretary was eliminated in early 1991, and a Parish Administrator was hired, Mrs. Judy Stockham. Her job has been to streamline the records and accounting, and with the help of a computer to keep the books for the treasurer. An addition to her job has been the handling of supermarket gift certificates (Dillon's stores in Kansas have made vouchers available to non-profit organizations to help them in fund-raising.) Outside the office, a new blue sign was placed on the Cathedral lawn, styled after those of English cathedrals. These and many other features of the Cathedral all contribute to its on-going goal of bringing more people to Christ.

There are many other items of interest that may have slipped between the cracks, but none intentionally. Many holy people have given their time, talent and treasure for the work of God at Christ Cathedral in Salina. To them is much appreciation owed, and to those who have departed this life, may they rest in peace.

EPILOGUE

One of the most difficult tasks for writers and editors of history is deciding when to end, finding a logical place to conclude. For no sooner does a book roll off the presses than it is already out of date. Such has been the case with the compilation of the history of Christ Cathedral. "Shall we end with a particular dean or bishop?" "Perhaps at the end of a calendar year?" "Can we make it current up to the date of publishing?" All these questions were considered as the printing date drew near. But unlike many of the histories the world has known, the Christian story (and therefore, the story of Christ Cathedral,) exists outside the bounds of time and space. Civilizations, wars and politics can all be narrowed to a certain time frame, but the Gospel goes on forever. So it will be with this book. We will pause now, in the middle of 1992, but the work of God at Christ Cathedral goes on. The people will change, the buildings will change, but the Faith of Jesus Christ will continue forever.

APPENDICES

Appendix A.
Memorials and Gifts

Stained glass windows:

Acolyte Room:
 Charles Fuge Lowder and
 James DeKoven   In memory of Jerry Anderson
 Bishop Grafton and   In thanksgiving for the Sisterhood
 Sister Agatha, SHN   of the Holy Nativity
 John Keble and Edward Pusey   In honor of Everet and Kyle Anderson

Choir Room:
 Choir of Angels   In memory of Phillip G. Rose
 150th Psalm   In memory of Harlan L. Hixon
 Nativity of Our Lord   In memory of Victor Tomlinson
 Crowning of King Solomon   In memory of Robert J. and Stella Anderson

Ladies' Room:
 St. Clare feeding the lepers   In memory of Marjorie M. Slaughter

St. Michael's Chapel:
 Holy Family   In memory of Harold Kinsley
 Deaconess and children   In memory of Deaconess Anne Gilliland
 Gethsemane and the Resurrection   In memory of departed Cathedral Clergy
 Ss. Michael and Nicholas   Christ Cathedral veterans memorial
 Jesus with children and
 The Last Supper   In memory of Jessie Lee Welch Paxton

Sacristy:
 Altar Guild   In memory of Marjorie Slaughter

North Transept:
 Baptism of Our Lord   In memory of Bishop and Mrs Robert H. Mize
 The Temptation of Christ   In memory of Isabel Menke
 Jesus Calming the Sea   In memory of the Seitz Family

South Transept:
    The Last Supper   In memory of John and Anna Kinkead
    Agony in the Garden   In memory of Willis Lowell Lindsey

Nave:
    Healing of the Cripple   In memory of Edwin B. and Laura R. Fish
    Woman at the Well   In thanksgiving by the Waddell Family
    Raising of Jairus' Daughter   In memory of Nellie Lee and Leonard C. Staples
    Entrance into Jerusalem   In memory of Charles, Grace and Kate Lee and Charlotte Lee Staples
    The Ascension   To the glory of God, by members and friends of Christ Cathedral

The Choir:
    St. Cecilia   In memory of Inez Julia Botsford
    The Crucifixion   In memory of William D. and Sarah Jane Lee
    St. Uriel   In memory of Mrs. Alfred Claflin
    The Resurrection   In memory of Cecil Florence Nichols Ritchie

Narthex:
    Christ the Light of the World   In memory of Arthur and Mabel DeBolt
    Christ the True Vine   In memory of Charles and Alice Schaaf
    Christ the Bread of Life   In memory of Bryan Hamilton Lynch
    Christ the Good Shepherd   In memory of Dr. Fred and Pearl Clark
    Glass around nave doors   In memory of James Henry Cannon

High Altar:
    Christ the King and Four Archangels,   To the Glory of God by members of
    Raphael, Michael, Gabriel, Uriel   the Cathedral

Other memorials and gifts in the Cathedral:

Sacred Vessels and liturgical fixtures:

    High Altar   In thanksgiving by Sarah Elizabeth Batterson
    High altar tabernacle   In memory of Bill Reed
    Sanctuary lamp   In memory of Don Noyes
    High Altar Cross   In memory of M.E.J.

Altar Cross at Mary Altar	In memory of Fr. Thomas B. and M.F. Dooley
Altar Cross in St. Michael's Chapel	In memory of Ellen L. Vail
Altar Cross	In memory of John Henry Hoover
Original wooden processional cross	From the estate of Fr. Hermon Batterson
Processional Cross	In memory of Bishop Sheldon Griswold
Glass Processional torches	In thanksgiving for their ordinations by Fr. Joseph Kimmett and Fr. James Cox
Wooden Processional torches	In memory of J.H. Winterbotham
High altar candlesticks	In thanksgiving by parishioners of Hudson, N.Y.: Mrs. S.B. Coffin, Mrs. O.H. Bradley, Mrs. R.W. Evans, Mrs. W.F. Holsapple and Miss M.H. Seymour
Gold, jeweled Communion set	In memory of Fr. Hermon and Sarah Batterson
Chalices and patens	In memory of Franklin Adams, Franklin Adams Jr. and Nette Ober Bren and in thanksgiving by H.L. and A.C.L.
Gold chalice and ciborium	In memory of Frankl Benedict Steifel
Ciborium	In memory of Earl James Richards
Candle snuffers	In memory of Dan and Bernice Kastner
Paschal candle stand	In memory of Wanda Lamar
Alms basin and Stand	In thanksgiving by the Women's Auxiliary, St. John's, Delhi, New York
Flower vases	In memory of Sallie Kirkland
Silver cruets	In memory of L.D. Merillat
Lavabo bowls	In memory of Elenor Hine and Warren and Louise Lee Welch
Bread boxes	In memory of Anderson D. and Mary Ann Hine and Warren T. and Louise Lee Welch
Sanctus bell	In memory of Elizabeth Farrell Buzick
Missal stand	In memory of Bernice Viola Clem
East holy water stoops	In memory of Mel Jarvis
North holy water stoops	In memory of Dr. Burton Osborn

Holy Books:

The first altar book	In thanksgiving by Bishop Sheldon Griswold
Gospel book	In memory of Harlan L. Hixon and Maude Kelly Deal

Bibles	In honor of Dean Frederic W. Litchman, priest, In memory of Dorothy Gertrude Keshner and Ruth Pomeroy Gibson
1928 Altar Missal	In memory of Joseph William Deal and Caroline Link Fischer
1979 Altar Missal	In memory of Maude Kelly Deal
The First Prayer Books and Hymnals	The New York Bible Society

Prayer Books and 1982 Hymnals, in memory of:

Ermyntrude Cunningham	Nelly N. Kellams	Mildred Selter
Polly Ellis	Leonard J. Lambert	Lewis W. Shollenberger Jr.
Janice Evans	Greg Lamone	Milo G. Sloo Jr.
Sue Gamble Fink	Lonnie Leisure	Bill Smith
Frances Floyd	Lois J. Noyes	Bill Stannard
Ida Hollis	Nellie Parry	Mildred Williams
Jane Hoobler	Lenore Reinsch	Kenneth L. Wright

Vestments and Linens:

First Altar Linen	In thanksgiving by the All Saints' Sisters
Holy day linens	In thanksgiving by the E.C.W.
The first Cathedral vestments	In thanksgiving by Deaconess Frances Kennett, E.T. Gerry, W.G. Read and St. Clement's, Philadelphia
Red Solemn Mass vestments	In memory of Kelly Slaughter
Blue Solemn Mass vestments	In thanksgiving
White Solemn Mass vestments	In memory of Martha Litchman
Green Solemn Mass vestments	In thanksgiving
Lenten array Mass vestments	In thanksgiving by Barbara Young
Altar frontal	In memory of Russ Guernsey and Beaulah Reese

Articles for use at special times:

Votive candle stands	In memory of Dale Lamar
Oil aumbry	In memory of Frances Brown, Kathryn Laughlin and Flora Nash
Mural at Baptismal font	In memory of Oscar and Johanna S. Seitz and Jacob and Wilhelmina Frank
Baptismal shell	In memory of Jessie Lee Paxton
Font liner	In memory of Geroge Rose and Elisha James White

Stand for Advent Wreath	In memory of Roy Ogden
Christmas Nativity Scene	In thanksgiving
Stations of the Cross	In thanksgiving by Fr. Willys Neustrom
American and Episcopal flags	In memory of James A. Hiller
Table for cremains	In memory of Adolph E. Brunner

Church Furnishings:

Sacristy	In memory of many faithful souls
Piscina in sacristy	In memory of Catherine Sturtavent
High Altar Triptych	In memory of Phillip G. Rose
Rood Screen	In memory of Sarah Elizabeth Batterson
Lectern	In memory of Bishop Thomas Hubbard Vail
Pulpit	In memory of Bishop Elisha Smith Thomas
High Altar Rail	In memory of Bishop Frank Rosebrook Millspaugh
Nave altar pace	In honor of Helen Litchman
Dean's Stall	In memory of Leslie Pell Clarke
Bishop's Throne	In thanksgiving for Bishop Griswold
Sedelia	In thanksgiving by Dean and Ernestine Kindlesparger
Carpeting	In thanksgiving by D.A. Norris
Chapel chandelier	In thanksgiving by Leonard Wood
Chapel furnishings	In thanksgiving by Thomas E. Synder
Nave chandeliers	In memory of Bryan Lynch
Hallway door	In thanksgiving
The first Altar Desk	In thanksgiving by Mrs. Samuel McCullagh
Original Litany Desk	From the estate of Fr. Hermon Batterson
Prayer desk	In memory of John Henry Hoover
Needlework	In thanksgiving by the women of the Cathedral
Ring pillow for weddings	In thanksgiving by Connie Whittaker and Betty Morgenstern
Chapel altar rail and needlework	In memory of Carole Johnson
Guest book stand	In memory of the parents of Hal and Bettie Kinsley
Altar Guild frame	In memory of Willis L. Lindsey
Tower bells	In memory of Arthur Claflin and Edgar Laubengayer
Piano	In memory of Ronald G. Beaudry
Choir Room Restoration	In memory of Harlan L. Hixon

Parish Hall:
    The Parish Hall — In memory of Henry Putnam
    Library — In memory of Martha Litchman
    Podium — In memory of George and Elizabeth W. Seitz Jr.
    Wooden Cross — In memory of Harold Kinsley
    Wooden chairs — In memory of Anderson David Hine

Education and Office Buidling:
    Room #1 and #9 — In memory of Jerry E. Anderson
    Room #2 — In memory of John L. Litchman
    Room #3 — In memory of Dean Donnon E. Strong, priest
    Room #4 — In memory of LaRue Royce
    Room #5 — In thanksgiving for Deaconess Anne Gilliland
    Room #6 — In memory of Addie Young
    Room #7 — In memory of Grace Wellington and E.A. Hiller
    Room #8 — In thanksgiving by Leo and Virginia Lambeth
    Room #10 — In memory of Richard W. King
    Room #11 — In memory of John Kirkland
    Room #12 — In memory of James A. Hiller

Outdoor memorials and gifts:
    Cathedral sign — In memory of the Wilmarth and Koons Families
    Outdoor Altar — In memory of Gerald N. Waddell
    Outdoor Stations of the Cross — In thanksgiving by Fr. and Mrs. Willys Neustrom
    Corpus on the 12th Station — In memory of Dean F.W. Litchman
    Statue of Mary — In honor of Our Lady, by the Society of Mary
    Poles and flags — In honor of Col. Keith G. Duckers
    Pear trees — In memory of Loren Slaughter
    Patio and lamp — In memory of Betty Roth
    Ninth Street Wall — In memory of Dean Frederic W. Litchman, priest
    Well and Sprinkler system — In thanksgiving

Boy Scout Eagle Projects:
    Cathedral Office sign — Scott Gafford
    Park benches — Shane Parker
    Garden bench — David Litchman
    Fence in parking lot — David Grittman

Memorial Park Gazebo, in memory of:

Jane Bradley	Florence Johnson	Helen Redding
Phil Bramwell	Sallie Kirkland	Frida Shoemaker
May Burch	Doris Kruckemyer	Lila Shanks
Edna Carey	John M. Lewis	Richard M. Smith
Shirley DeChant	Opal Merillat	Muriel Summer
Oliver DeWolf	May Norris	Gerald N. Waddell
Barbara Faupel	Harry Ogden	Beatrice Woodward
Barbara Foret	Arthur J. Rathbun Sr.	Earl C. Woodward
Elizabeth Gearse		

Appendix B.
Ordinations in Christ Cathedral

	Position	Date	Bishop
Adams, Charles Laurence	Priest	28 Feb 1904	Griswold
Anderson, Augustine H.W.	Priest	29 Sept 1904	Griswold
Chapman, Samuel Andrew	Priest	30 Nov 1909	Griswold
Sargent, Clarence Spalding	Deacon	17 July 1910	Griswold
Holsapple, Lloyd Burdwin	Priest	21 Sept 1910	Griswold
Inwood, Norman	Priest	21 Dec 1910	Griswold
Virden, Harry Lee	Deacon	23 Nov 1913	Griswold
Merrill, Edwin Walter	Priest	21 Dec 1913	Griswold
Sparks, Thomas Ayers	Priest	21 Dec 1913	Griswold
Prout, Frank Rice	Priest	21 Dec 1915	Griswold
Miller, Alfred Gilliland	Priest	6 Mar 1918	Sage
Myers, Frank Ruben	Deacon	5 Jan 1919	Sage
Myers, Frank Ruben	Priest	18 Oct 1919	Beecher
Smith, Stanley Lawrence	Deacon	8 June 1921	Mize
Lyons, Samuel Francis	Deacon	25 Sept 1921	Mize
Weaver, Vernon Alban	Deacon	25 Sept 1921	Mize
Reynolds, Francis Core	Deacon	25 Sept 1921	Mize
Reynolds, Francis Core	Priest	18 Oct 1922	Mize
Smith, Stanley Lawrence	Priest	7 June 1925	Mize
Gibbons, Joseph William	Deacon	25 Sept 1925	Mize
Botkin, Warren Loring	Deacon	27 Dec 1925	Mize
Seitz, Oscar Jacob Frank	Deacon	27 Dec 1925	Mize
Barnes, William	Deacon	27 Dec 1925	Mize
Barnes, William	Priest	27 June 1926	Mize
Kennedy, Harry Sherbourne	Priest	27 June 1926	Mize
Hughbanks, Leroy	Deacon	11 June 1929	Mize
Mize, Edward Moore	Deacon	8 June 1930	Mize
Mize, Edward Moore	Priest	17 Dec 1930	Mize
Greismeyer, Orin Anthony	Deacon	31 May 1931	Mize
Maurer, John Dean	Deacon	19 Dec 1934	Mize
Maurer, John Dean	Priest	16 Mar 1936	Mize
Clem, Remy Leland	Priest	4 May 1941	Nichols
Weeman, Gordon William	Priest	20 Sept 1942	Nichols
Francis, Peter	Priest	18 Oct 1944	Nichols
Miller, Poland Howard	Deacon	23 Sept 1945	Nichols

Hotaling, Wilfred Eugene	Priest	23 Sept 1951	Nichols
Staples, Austin Joyce	Priest	29 May 1953	Nichols
Atkinson, Clifford William	Priest	29 May 1953	Nichols
Jones, Marx Arthur	Priest	22 Dec 1953	Nichols
Feallock, Richard Arthur	Deacon	24 Sept 1958	Lewis
Warthan, Frank A.	Deacon	5 Oct 1975	Davidson
Martin, George Lee	Deacon	15 Aug 1982	Ashby
Lambert, Sally A.	Deacon	18 June 1983	Ashby
McConkey, David Benton	Deacon	29 Oct 1983	Ashby
Tilson, Alan	Deacon	29 June 1984	Ashby
McConkey, David Benton	Priest	11 July 1984	Ashby
Tilson, Alan	Priest	5 Jan 1985	Ashby
Null, J. Ashley	Deacon	31 Aug 1985	Ashby
Cox, James Richard	Deacon	26 May 1990	Ashby
Cox, James Richard	Priest	30 Nov 1990	Ashby
Kimmett, Joseph Marshall	Priest	7 Dec 1990	Ashby

Appendix C.
Wardens

Year	Senior Warden	Junior Warden
1870	Mr. James Chase	Mr. J.H. Prescott

When the local parish was dissolved and a Cathedral Chapter formed, the local members of the Chapter served as the parish vestry.

At the Annual Meeting of 1937, Dean Hewitt Vinnedge reported that most of the early records of Christ Church and Christ Cathedral had been lost. Until the 1960's, Chapter minutes and newsletters indicate parishioners who served on the vestry, but not always which men were wardens.

Year	Senior Warden	Junior Warden
1922	Edwards A. Hiller	Leonard Staples
1925	Edwards A. Hiller	J.H. Winterbotham
1940-42	Fred C. Utt	Anson Jordan
1946-51	Fred C. Utt	G.N. Waddell
1952	Fred C. Utt	Phil Rose

In 1953 a change was made in the Cathedral by-laws so that the Senior Warden was appointed by the Dean and the Junior (or "Peoples") Warden was elected. Fred C. Utt was commended for thirty-eight years of service and given the title Senior Warden Emeritus.

Year	Senior Warden	Junior Warden
1954		Kelly Slaughter
1955	G.N Waddell	Hal Kinsley
1956		Dan Kastner
1957	Whitley Austin	G.E. Anderson
1958	G.E. Anderson	Leonard Wood
1959	Leonard Wood	
1960	Andy Young	W.C. Chaffee
1961	Willis Bell	W. Baxter
1962	J.G. Williamson	John Williams
1963	J.G. Williamson	Keith Oliver
1964	Keith Oliver	Kelly Slaughter
1965	Kelly Slaughter	Keith Duckers
1966	Kelly Slaughter	Jim Dowell
1967	Robert Weber	R.L. Guernsey

1968	Robert Weber	James Roderick
1969	James Roderick	Frank Stockham
1970	James Roderick	Larry Shoffner
1971	Dick George	Robert Kastner
1972	Robert Kastner	J.D. Rector
1973	J.G. Williamson	Robert Anderson
1974	Loran Slaughter	Robert Anderson
1975	David Lasley	James McCoy
1976	James McCoy	Vernon Osborn
1977	Vernon Osborn	Richard McMullin
1978	Milo Sloo	William Grosser, Jr.
1979	Milo Sloo	William Grosser, Jr.
1980	Milo Sloo	Mike Brown
1981	John Williamson, Mike Brown	Mike Brown
1982	Reese Baxter	Monte Allen
1983	Reese Baxter	Tom Snyder
1984	Robert Frisbie	Tom Snyder
1985	Robert Frisbie	Tom Snyder
1986	Robert Frisbie	Tom Snyder
1987	Leonard Wood	Douglas Miller
1988	Margarette Parker, Ray Freeman	Sara Cassetty
1989	Ray Freeman	Barbara Young
1990	Steve Bressler	Barbara Young
1991	Robert Kastner	Carolyn Peterson
1992	Roger Brent	Steve Hays

Resources

Published Sources:

Abbeys, Castles, Great Houses and Gardens in Britain, Georgaphia Ltd., London.
As We Were; A Pictorial History of Saline County, Saline County Historical Society, Salina, 1976.
The Book of Common Prayer, 1928 and 1979.
First 100 Years of the Diocese of Kansas, Allen Press, Lawrence, Kansas, 1964.
The Spirit of Missions, The Domestic and Foreign Missionary Society, New York.
Baedeker, Karl, *Great Britain; Handbook for Travellers, Vol. 1.*, Macmillan, New York, 1966.
Barnds, William J., *The Episcopal Church in Nebraska; A Centennial History*, Diocese of Nebraska, Omaha, 1969.
Bramwell, Ruby Phillips, *City on the Move; The Story of Salina*, Survey Press, Salina, 1969.
Brewster, H. Pomeroy, *Saints and Festivals of the Christian Church*, Frederick A. Stokes Co., Gale Reprint CO., 1974.
Cross, F.L. and Livingstone, E.A., editors, *Oxford Dictionary of the Christian Church*, Oxford University Press, 1974.
Ferguson, George, *Signs and Symbols in Christian Art*, Oxford University Press, 1966.
Ghirsham, Minorsky and Sanghvi, *Persia; The Immortal Kingdom*, New York Graphic Society, New York, 1971.
Neal, Emily Gardiner, *Father Bob and His Boys*, The Bobbs-Merrill Co. Inc., Indianapolis, 1963.
Neil, William, editor, *The Bible Companion*, McGraw Hill, New York, 1960.
Talbot, William L., *St. John's Church in Keokuk; A History, 1850-1975*, St. John's Church, Keokuk, Iowa, 1975.
Wilson, Peter L., *Angels*, Pantheon Books, New York, 1980.

Periodicals:

The Cathedral Age, Irving & Casson, A.H. Davenport Co., New York, Vol. XI, No. 4, Winter 1936-37.
Crossroads, Vol. 43, No. 1, 1967.
Forth, The Spirit of Missions, Vol. CV, No 10, October 1940.
The Living Church, Milwaukee, Wisconsin.
Rochester Democrat and Chronicle, Rochester, New York.
Rochester Times-Union, Rochester, New York.

The Salina Evening Journal, Salina, Kansas.
The Salina Journal, Salina, Kansas.
The Salina-Union, Salina, Kansas.
Weaver, Glenn, *The Society for the Increase of Ministry; A Centenary History*, reprinted from the Historical Magazine of the Episcopal Church, December, 1957.
The Wichita Beacon, Wichita, Kansas

Other Resources:
Batterson Geneological Records, Microfiche IGI-M0023, Mormon Library and Archives, Salt Lake City, Utah.
Wooster, L.D., "Some Early History of Boy Scouting in the Salina to Hays Area", BSA, Coronado, 1957.
Where We Are and How We Got Here, St. Francis Boys' Home, Salina, 1975.
American Church Clergy and Parish Directory, ed. Lloyd, 1903.
Clerical Directory of the (Protestant) Episcopal Church, Church Hymnal Corporation, New York.
Episcopal Church Annual, Morehouse-Gorham, New York.
Stowe's Clerical Directory, Church Hymnal Corporation, New York.

The Missionary District of Salina, of Western Kansas and the Diocese of Western Kansas:

1903-1932	*The District of Salina Watchman*
1937	*The New Watchman*
1938-1955	*The Watchman*
1956	*Newsletter*
1964-1965	*Bishop's Newsletter of the Missionary District of Western Kansas*
1967	*Your Episcopal Church*
1968-1969	*The Newsletter of the Episcopal Church in the Missionary District of Western Kansas,*
1970-1972	*The Newsletter of the Episcopal Church in the Diocese of Western Kansas*
1972-1975	*Newsletter*
1976-1981	*The Episcopalian / Western Kansas Newsletter*
1981-	*The Prarie Spirit*

The Archives of Christ Cathedral:
The Cathedral News, The Weekly Chimes, The Cathedral Chimes, The Cathedral Times as well as minutes of the Chapter and Vestry, parish organizations, bulletins, brochures, service registers, annual reports and sermon transcripts.

ACKNOWLEDGEMENTS

The Editors

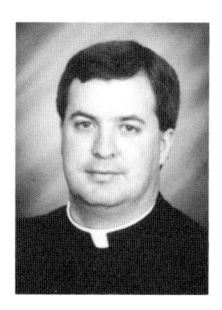

Joseph M. Kimmett
Fr. Kimmett is a native of Denver, Colorado. He graduated from the University of Colorado in 1984 and Nashotah House in 1990. He is Canon in Residence at Christ Cathedral.

Jo Reed
A native of Oklahoma, Jo Kenworthy Reed has degrees from Marymount College in Salina and Kansas State University. She teaches high school English in Salina and has been a member of the Cathedral since 1961.

We wish to acknowledge the people who contributed to this historical account of Christ Cathedral. Through archival research, personal recall, interviews and correspondence, they uncovered information that might have otherwise been lost. This production would never have been possible without their diligence.

Whitley Austin
Roger H. Brent
Mary-Eliot Craig
Jody Dennett
Elizabeth Duckers
Marilyn Dowell
Robert J. Falta
Lila Hammond
M. Richard Hatfield
Sharon Kidwell
Jack Lambert
Sally Lambert
Robert Luehrs
David McConkey
Ethel McCoy

Edith Morse
J. Ashley Null
Sophia Osborn
Margarette Parker
Harris Rayl
Nancy Roderick
Virginia Rose
John Q. Royce
Teresa Snyder
Joyce White
Norman Wilkinson
Sally Wilkinson
Nell Wood
Royce Young

To those outside the Cathedral who helped:
Elaine J. Cocordas, Philadelphia
Lois Gould, Hudson, New York
Elinor Hearne, Austin, Texas

Mrs. Frank Hubble, Albuquerque
Margaret Stavridi
Charles J. Yeske, Doylestown, Pennsylvania

Our photographers:
Roger H. Brent
Robert J. Falta
Phil Hegel
Chris Jambor
Arlene D. Kimmett
Joseph M. Kimmett
Paul Neis

John Q. Royce
Royce Young

Additional photographs are courtesy of:
The Cathedral Archives
Saint Francis Academy
Saint John's Military School
Archives of the Diocese of Kansas

Special thanks to our typist and computer consultant, Judith Schneider.